125 Years of Serving

1886-2011

Table of Contents

M.T. Publishing Company, Inc.™
P.O. Box 6802
Evansville, Indiana 47719-6802
www.mtpublishing.com

Copyright © 2011
Plano Fire Department
All rights reserved.

Library of Congress Control Number:
2011939614

ISBN: 978-1-934729-74-8

Graphic Design and Pre-Press by
M.T. Publishing Company, Inc.

Out of 200 Commemorative Editions printed, this book is number **17**.

P.O. Box 860358 Plano, Texas 75086-0358
972-941-7000   www.plano.gov

January 2012

Citizens and Readers:

The year 2011 marked the 125th anniversary of the Plano Fire Department; 125 years of dedicated, loyal service to the people of Plano, Texas. Very much like our city, the Fire Department has a rich history that started on land that once teemed with farms and dirt roads. While Plano has grown into a modern, vibrant, urban city, home to some of America's most successful corporate headquarters, the Fire Department has grown and evolved from wooden ladders, oxygen resuscitators and cotton-jacketed fire hose to enclosed air-conditioned fire apparatus, LifePak 15 defibrillators and advanced therapeutic life-saving medical services.

It is a sincere privilege and pleasure to foreword this pictorial history of the Plano Fire Department; the department I am very proud to lead as Fire Chief and that lists as a few of its hallmarks great community support, forward thinking and innovation, leading edge technologies, outstanding training and equipment, strong leadership and the finest firefighters in the nation. It is these hallmarks that the department has used to build an exemplary fire and EMS provider. To date, the Plano Fire Department is the only ISO Class 1 fire department in the world that also holds international accreditations in fire suppression through the Center for Public Safety Excellence and ambulance service through the Commission on Ambulance Accreditation Service.

The following 200 pages will take the reader from the black and white images of a small volunteer department to the colored photographs of a modern, state-of-the-art fire department that is a key member of our Plano community in 2011. The first 125 years of our existence are memorialized in these pages and the courage, integrity, and dedication to duty is reflected in the men and women who served in the past, serve now and will serve in the Plano Fire Department for the next 125 years. Please enjoy the book and join our department as we celebrate our storied past and look enthusiastically to the future.

Sincerely,

Hugo R. Esparza
Fire Chief

Plano Fire Department
1901 Avenue K, Plano, TX 75074
www.planofire.org

Phil Dyer
Mayor

Pat Miner
Mayor Pro Tem

Lissa Smith
Deputy Mayor Pro Tem

Ben Harris
Place 2

André Davidson
Place 3

Plano Fire Chiefs

1887	J. A. Moreman
	(The Eclipse Fire Company)
1894	John O. Gates
1897	Ralph Wyatt
1898	E. O. Harrington
1911 ~ 1920	Gee Hudson
1920 ~ 1930	R. B. Howey
1931	Jim Griffin
1939 ~ 1950	Jim Standerfer
1951	John Dean
1952 ~ 1955	B. Garrett
1956	John Garrett
1958	C. C. Oliver
1959 ~ 1962	J. R. Dupree
1964	Bill Gentry
1965	John Dean
1966 ~ 1982	Lee Mayfield
1982 ~ 2006	Bill Peterson
2006	Hugo Esparza

Plano Fire Department Personnel ~ 2011

by Rank, Seniority, and Hire Date

Fire Chief

Hugo R. Esparza

Assistant Chiefs

Alan Storck
Jimmy Dickerson
David Kerr
Dan Thompson

Battalion Chiefs

Robert Fickling
Jonathan Everett
Michael Shafer
Billy Lay
John Cardwell
Danny Burks
Kelly Helm
Forest Harrell
Martin Wade

Captains

F. Jeff Amadon
Scott Kerr
Robert Mason
Jack Sides
Roy Brockway
Jimmy Doan
Jason Summers
Gary Gray
Steven Sanders
Ronald Cooper
Gayland Gibbs
Mark Scott
James Benton
Matthew Nelson
Toby Peacock
Randy Stone
Allen Light
Kenneth Klein
Kevin Wilkerson
Jennifer Maxwell
Floyd Jones
Christopher Bechtold
Shawn Price
Greg Beck
Mark Vice
Brent Overman
Damon Smith
Kevin Dritschler
Chris Biggerstaff
Les Ruble

Scott Mammel
Eric Wahlberg
Joel Harper
Scott Mallen
Steven Poe
Peggy Harrell
Marc Pate
David Hill
Shawn Childress
Anthony Aspden
Anthony Gray

Lieutenants

Mark Hardy
Michael Malone
Stan Lawing
Paul Paredez
Daniel Anderson
Daniel Rogers
Terry Beck
Jason Tubb
Brian Kanzaki
Jack Miller
Daniel Moore
John Vike
Harding Woolsey
Michael Vernon
Brice Nowell
Kelly Tomlin

Richie Floyd
Kade Wallace
Jaime Reyes
Jeffrey Capehart
Timothy Taylor

Fire Apparatus Operators

David Edwards
Gerald Becker
James Frock
James Pecky
Michael Ussery
Russell Presley
Joe Hooten
Charles O'Shel
John Kirby
Richard Sherard
Philip Nation
Roger Nunneley
John Burch
Larry Armstrong
Edward Harris
Donald Gladney
William Ripley
Dudley Blackburn
Stephen Borski
Gerald Walters

Tony Hardie
Gary Glenn
Matthew Schira
Brian Ingram
Roger Andrews
Timothy O'Connor
Trey Thurston
Deanne Murillo
Kelly Kuropata
James Schooling
Wilson Spain
Chris Patterson
Chris Mougia
Joseph Simmons
Eric Burks
Michael Carr
Stacy Cagle
Raymond Fitch
Monte Allred
Kenny Braley
Bobby Cole
Matthew Higginbotham
Mathieu Frajkor
Karry Gafford
Ryan Clark
Aaron Deary
Robert Hogan
Larry Combest
Paul Aldred
Jeffrey Moberley

Fire Rescue Specialists

Terry King
Allen West
Clifford Dicken
Mark Nugent
Calvin Cook
James Hamm
Ronald Gregory
John Nerwich
Allan Rasor
Mark Shields
Danny Decker
Robert York
Mark Barnett
Randall Jones
Robert Papin
Robert Hawkins
William Swaner
Joe Flores
Ronald Rawlings
Brenda Mammel
Michael Covey
James Henry
Patricia Swavey
David Abshier
Roy Weed
Brian Shelton
Phillip Crombie
Robert Walker
Anthony Brown
David Corbett
Harold Wilson
Darren Hagan

Bradley Matocha
Christopher Jefferson
Trent Bedford
Jeffrey Bates
Bryan Moeller
Kenneth Southard
John Whitehead
Anthony Christian
Michael Boatman
Michael Sweeney
James Pitts
Jonathan Hokit
James Joiner
Steven Reynolds
Aaron Kelly
Eric Everson
Robert Grant
David Engle
Michael Waterstradt
Clark Baker
Arturo Lujan
Dwayne Shelby
Kevin Haines
Marco Banuelas
Ricky Nevil
Stephen Finley
Clinton Foster
Gary Miller
Alberto Valdez
Ronald Robertson
Holly Mischnick
David Harris
David Looney
Ronald Gall
Matthew Nichter
Phillip Hazelip
Donald Sherer
Alan Nicholson
Ronnie Hargrave
Mark Pollard
Lee Jennings
Michael Lewis
Lindy Lawley
Kevin Hargrove
Jason Massingill
Matthew Brewer
Jeffrey Bell
Aaron Clouse
Gerald Majka
Steven King
Jeffrey Stevens
Bryan Addington
John Hood
Michael Stubblefield
Jeffrey Deskeere
Brian Stroven
William Isaacs
David Schott
Keil Baldia
Keith Wallace
Kyle Crayton
Joel Hall
Jason McGraw
Shaun Richey
Chad Holm

Anthony Hostutler
John Criswell
Wesley Armstrong
Clinton McAdoo
Cody Cox
Joseph Keifer
James Walker
John Holland
Clinton Smith
Cody Gray
Clayton Lane
Michael Tartaro
Jeffrey Quinn
Randy Wood
Jeffrey Kendrick
Laddin Gillespie
Troy Berry
Christopher Larue
Jesse Coon
Fletcher Farris
Stephen Sheffield
Christopher Owens
Christopher Willits
Mark Long
Jared Barker
Richard Leidig
David Reichert
Christopher Lammons
Bradford McCutcheon
Nicholas Kalina
Samuel McDonald
James Harris
John Askew
Matthew Sutphin
Nathan Fisk
Daniel Alexander
Dennis Gieseker
Nathan Daniels
Brent Cuba
Beau Simpson
Matthew Gaston
Brian Trammell
Kenneth Carpenter
Jeremy Treadway
Joel Fernandes
Bryan Buchanan
Justin Samuel
Jeffrey Lindsey
Steven Huth
Brandon Whitney
Brandon Williams
Patrick Amoroso
Patrick Dunn
Kyle Yeck
Craig Westwood
Anthony Pospick
Jeremy Vandagriff
Daniel Daly
Andrew Scates
Jeremy Wilkinson
Alexander Shahandeh
Wesley Campbell
Joshua Ferrell
Jarrett Beshears
Brian Belcher

Aaron Hale
Bradford Scofield
Michael Matej
Phillipe Talley
Douglas Looney
Anthony DiMarco
John Weatherby
Eric Goldberg
Timothy Melton
Jonathan Lindsey
John Barrett
Steven Thimons
Steven Grogan
Shane Vaughan
Ryan Strutton
Thomas Cullum
Joshua Pitcox
Grayson Sanders
Steven Tuck
Coy Mathis
Tyler Herring
David Armstrong
Manuel Duarte
Nicholas Bottoms
Justin Ferguson
Stephen Grammer
Mark Guerra
Shawn Hammond
Adam Arthur
Kyle Moore
Shaun Batey
Brody Fleming
Micah Shipley
Steven Mears

Administrative Staff

Frank Snidow,
Budget Analyst
Todd Ramage,
Senior Programmer/Analyst
Samuel Grissom,
Programmer/Analyst II
Cynthia Morgan,
Administrative Coordinator
Jason Gregorash,
Research Analyst

Senior Administrative Assistants

Lori Holter
Pat Baxter
Jennifer Bradley
Teresa Burris
Sonora Copling
Sherry Chance-Parrish

Administrative Assistant

Jacqueline Ellis
Barbara Winchester

They stand on the corner of Main and Mechanic in their Sunday best, assembled in a comfortable stance that speaks of their obvious camaraderie. In front is the eager young man who volunteered to head the line, enjoying his first photographic experience. Behind him is the confident cigar smoker, out of place with his movie star looks and civil war officer's hat. Next is the young boy trying his best to strike a rakish pose to surprise the girls, cigar in hand, a solemn look of authority on his face. From the mustachioed mill operator to the portly grocer to the suspender-wearing delivery man, these ten men pose for the camera, never imagining over 130 years later their eyes would be staring into yours, the past looking into the future, the future gazing back into the past.

This newly discovered photograph is believed to be the first record of an organized Plano fire suppression team, pre-dating the City's 1887 first recorded bucket brigade. They stand in the dusty roadway of what is now Avenue K and 15th Street, the footprint of the building façade still visible today. They pose to the sound of wagons and mules, the shrill whistle of the cotton gin and heavy boots on wooden sidewalks, now replaced by the hum of the electric rail and the music and laughter of late night diners as evening comes alive in historic Downtown Plano.

"The ultimate test of a man's conscience may be his willingness to sacrifice something today for future generations whose words of thanks will not be heard," said politician Gaylord Nelson. These ten men lived that creed as do the members of today's Plano Fire Department.

DEDICATION

This glimpse at the history of Plano's Fire Department as it celebrates its 125th anniversary is dedicated to the firefighters who have protected and enhanced the quality of life in Plano over the decades of time. It is dedicated to the citizens who fired pistols in the air as a call to arms when a fire broke out – defying the odds with buckets of water and determined grit. It is dedicated to the organized volunteers who learned to fight fires with hoses spilling from a truck they rigged up on a used chassis they purchased after a community fundraiser.

It is dedicated to the men and women of today's department who, armed with computers, code books, education, investigative, medical and fire suppression training, are still defying the odds with water and determination. It is dedicated to those who are willing to sacrifice something today, *for future generations whose words of thanks will not be heard.*

Foreword

They mainly came from Tennessee and Kentucky, settlers hooking their futures to a Conestoga and a plow. They sought out the rich blackland soils of Collin County, some arriving as early as 1845, traveling by the hundreds on the established wagon trail now known as Preston Road. Some came to escape the ravages of the Civil War, which had left lands desolate and businesses in ruins, some came to join family who sent encouraging letters about abundant opportunity. All, however, came with a common goal – to carve success out of the wildly independent new state of Texas.

As neighbors in scattered settlements embraced common needs and interests, they began to form the foundation for the social and economic hub that became known as the City of Plano. Incorporated in June 1873 it was named for the mistaken Spanish word for "plains." Farms were flourishing by then with churches and schools moving from their humble beginnings in homes and cabins to newly constructed buildings "in town." Merchants arrived, doubling in number as the railroad worked its way through the countryside into Dallas, then tripling in number as cotton and corn made Plano an agricultural king. The strong fiber of community formed the vibrant social, economic and political fabric of sustained growth.

The 1880's saw a bustling town with settler memories recording a four-horse stage kicking up clouds of dust as the mail was delivered. Roads were beaten out of cow trails on the prairie with the streets of Plano unpaved and downtown lined with wooden buildings and plank sidewalks. At times over 30 wagons would be lined up to unload grain onto the waiting boxcars of the Houston and Texas Central rail. Gins and gristmills sprang up to handle the rich harvest of the blackland soil. Merchants included the furniture maker who doubled as the undertaker, grocers, dry goods, barbers, liveries, restaurants, lumber, shoe and drug stores, attorneys, a newspaper, no less than three saloons and a billiard hall.

There was intrigue as well. Notorious outlaw Sam Bass undertook the first train robbery in Texas just six miles north of Plano in 1878 after being welcomed as a stranger in need at the Wells farm in Plano the night before. Passengers were reportedly so surprised they didn't know whether to give chase or applaud. Frank and Jesse James often visited a local farm with the Younger gang. Bandit queen Belle Starr was inadvertently welcomed as a traveler in need of shelter by the Clint Haggard family who even invited her and a companion to a square dance. A strange blend of peddlers, roving medicine shows and traveling salesmen wove in and out of daily life. The last of the

great buffalo herds and an occasional band of Cherokee could still be sighted. It was into this rich mixture of the traditional old west and the coming constraints of civilization that the Plano Fire Department sunk its roots.

The morning of August 27, 1881, Plano's entire business district burned to the ground. Livestock was saved and little else. Only a single saloon was left, enjoying a brisk business in the coming weeks. A testament to the tenacity of the community, the following day a tent city sprang up in the ash-strewn roadway to house people and supplies as the community rebuilt. With reconstruction soon underway, the City Council proclaimed only brick veneer could be utilized on exteriors to reduce the spread of fire.

The Act of 1875 was chewed on and not passed by the Texas legislature until ten years later, but in 1885 the Act of 1875 broadened the rights of individual cities, including permission to organize fire brigades. With multiple damaging fires continuing to plague downtown with its conjoined structures, the City Council immediately took action under the Act, approving the services of Plano's first recorded fire brigade, June 14, 1887.

Headed by local businessman, J. A. Moreman, the Eclipse Fire Company came to life. Recognizing that fire and economic success were not good partners, many prominent businessmen urged the City Council to continue fire suppression action.

June 1887: Eclipse Fire Company is formed. *September 1887: O. Davis Hook and Ladder Company* debuts its newly purchased wagon. *December 1887:* A shed is built to house the fire apparatus with a special tax passed to help retire indebtedness for fire equipment purchases. *September 1890:* A well is dug at the intersection of Main and Mechanic (K Avenue and 15th) for the sole purpose of fighting fires. *January 1891:* A hand operated pump is purchased and mounted on a two-wheeled cart. *November 1893:* A hand drawn chemical engine is purchased along with 200 feet of hose, known as the *S. M. Harrington Chemical Company*, businessman Harrington among those championing its cause.

In February 1894 the City Council purchased land for the construction of a city hall to include a calaboose, room for the fire equipment and a livery for

the eventual purchase of fire horses. As the need for fire suppression expanded with the growth of the city, it was left to the community to furnish the necessary manpower and spunk. Loosely organized and largely untrained, enthusiastic volunteers ran the gauntlet from the Mayor to businessmen, the trash cart driver, gin operators, educators, ministers and local farmers. All equally responded to the fire alarm, three pistol shots fired in rapid succession.

A remembrance from 1894 recounts parishioners exiting the Christian Church to the sounds of pistols and the cry of "Fire!" Men ran in every direction as it was ascertained the local "college" was

aflame. Pulling the hand wagons through the rutted streets lined with mules, horses and buggies, a motley crew of volunteers struggled with suction hoses, pumps and buckets. The pump wagon almost immediately gave out but the newly acquired chemical engine was credited with saving several adjacent houses.

Saturday morning, October 26, 1895, held the promise for a beautiful autumn day. Many were planning to ride the rails into Dallas to see the latest wonders at the State Fair and to cheer on the large contingency of world-class Plano mules. By 5 am farmers were already loading their wagons with gins and businesses preparing for an early opening in anticipation of a brisk trades day. At 6 am the Mayor of Dallas was pushing back from the breakfast table when a call arrived saying Plano was in flames. An engine and company was hastily loaded onto a rail car, arriving at 8 am to find the wells were dry and the town was gone.

An unpublished poem tells of the anguish. "Our stores are rapidly burning down, nothing left but ashes, out on the ground. Our homes across the way so cosy and neat, cannot resist the terrible heat..the sparks by the millions, both large and small, are firing roofs as they continue to fall...Our wells are dry, our cisterns are dryer, we are left to the mercy of this terrible fire."

Once again the Plano community rolled up its sleeves, with the now familiar tents in the streets appearing as commerce continued and rebuilding got underway. As wooden sidewalks and awnings began to line the streets, more than one frame structure could be seen lurking behind the veneer storefronts. Alarmed, several merchants and citizens met with City Council urging enforcement and complete prohibition of wooden or corrugated iron wall buildings within the fire limits of Plano. Their petition was denied and when the rooster crowed the following morning 19 buildings in downtown had burned from a spark that had ignited a frame kitchen. Enough said. An ordinance was passed March 9, 1897, prohibiting wooden awnings in the downtown area.

Enough cannot be said about the early "fire boys," as they were called. At the sound of the pistols, they bolted from their sleep, ran from church services, left customers at the cash register, plows in the fields and ran to the fire shed. They gathered equipment, hoisted up the heavy wagons and headed out, often guided to their destination only by the plumes of smoke billowing in the air. They ran through rutted, muddy roadways, often coated with ice, as they strained to navigate the hand pulled wagons to the fire. The chemical wagon was especially effective in fire suppression and they had learned from trial and error how to mix bi-carbonate of soda into the water tank adding sulfuric acid at the scene to create the pressure that forced the liquid mixture through their one-inch hose. They were unpaid, had no uniforms and often arrived home covered in soot nursing broken arms, cuts and strained backs.

Following the March 1897 fire, the City Council was met with a petition May 11, 1897, requesting a number of citizens be recognized as The Plano Fire Company. There was little hesitation in honoring the request and that evening Ralph Wyatt sat down to dinner with his family as Plano's first Fire Chief. S. M. Harrington and several others championed for the purchase of a fire bell to be used as a fire alarm. The bell was immediately ordered, despite its extravagant cost of $57.50, placed atop a wooden tower. Pistol shots became a thing of the past. Members of the department were allowed to sleep in the newly opened City Hall, and 1,000 feet of hose was pur-

chased. Chief Wyatt recorded his first official report December 14, 1897, and by the following June the City was funding $2 per month for two teams to have organized training twice monthly.

There was great excitement in the community on a blustery day in March 1899. "Here they come!," cried a boy as he ran towards the livery at City Hall. Applause and cheers greeted the arrival of a team of jet black fire horses being led down Mechanic Street, their groomed coats glistening, manes billowing in the wind. Dan and Dude were the first team to be used by the department, the manually pulled wagons having been converted at a cost of $100 to accommodate harness. The team was partially funded by the city with additional funds coming from the community who supported various plays and minstrel shows facilitated by the department. Other teams eventually joined Dan and Dude, but they became legendary throughout the region for their prowess and went into the books as the best team the department ever owned.

1899 also heralded the first electricity in Plano. By 1901 lights were not only placed in the sleeping rooms at city hall, but the ringing of a telephone was now heard echoing through the corridors. In 1902 George Goode became the first salaried man on the fire department roster, agreeing to the care and feeding of Dan and Dude for the sum of $5 and a one-year exemption from street repair duty. In February 1904 the City Council decided to retain a permanent individual to stay at city hall. Dag Hudson entered the history books as Plano's first paid on-duty fireman, entering service in March 1904, remaining until June 1928.

While officially recognized as a fire department, with the exception of Dag Hudson all other firefighters remained on volunteer status, supplementing their equipment purchases and other efforts with fundraisers, donations and small apportionments from the city coffers. Almost beyond belief, as the Beatles were coming into

prominence at the Cavern Club in Liverpool, England and the space program was preparing to put a man on the moon, the Plano Fire Department was still operating with volunteer staffing.

On a frosted winter's night, January 4, 1911, the Plano Star Courier offices burned to the ground. Employed by the Courier, fire company secretary Will Jackson had determined their secure location in the "fire-proof building" would be ideal for the retention of records and photographs collected to date. All was lost, but the Courier credited the department stating, "The heroes of many fires in the past did some of the most valiant service ever done in the history of this city to save the entire town from going up in smoke." Today it is the stories handed down through generations, personal photographs, newspaper and municipal records that provide us the rich history of the Plano Fire Department's early beginnings. While the physical history of the department was destroyed, its spirit was not.

As you enjoy this 125th anniversary pictorial celebration of the department's history it will quickly become quickly evident the footprint of yesterday is the blueprint for today. Stalls are no longer cleaned, but equipment bays are hosed and swept. Teams are no longer hitched as livery doors are flung open but motors hum as bay doors rise. The fire bell no longer rings but the radio dispatches a first alarm. Stove pipes are no longer inspected for the proverbial flaw in the flue but hundreds of lives are saved by the provision of free batteries and smoke alarms during home inspections.

The past is behind, learn from it. The future is ahead, prepare for it. The present is here, live it.

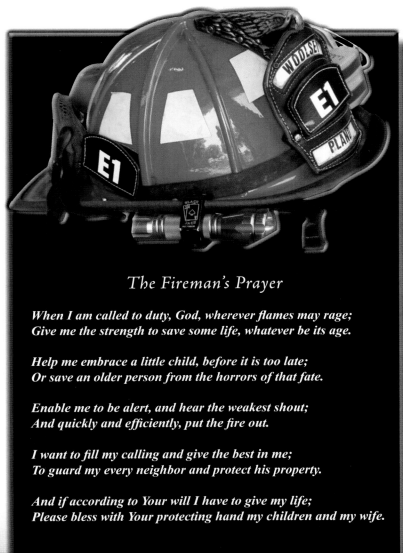

The Fireman's Prayer

When I am called to duty, God, wherever flames may rage;
Give me the strength to save some life, whatever be its age.

Help me embrace a little child, before it is too late;
Or save an older person from the horrors of that fate.

Enable me to be alert, and hear the weakest shout;
And quickly and efficiently, put the fire out.

I want to fill my calling and give the best in me;
To guard my every neighbor and protect his property.

And if according to Your will I have to give my life;
Please bless with Your protecting hand my children and my wife.

FIRE HISTORY RESCUE

By 1891 Plano was a thriving community and center of commerce for many small settlements in Collin County. It boasted a Mayor and City Council, rail access, a city marshal and calaboose, numerous private schools and several churches. There were dentists, physicians and attorneys. Cotton gins harvested the rich rewards of the blackland soil and a wide assortment of mercantiles lined downtown. Women could purchase the latest fashions at the millinery shoppe and a "sit down dinner" could be found at the boarding house restaurant. The local bar and billiard room raised more than one minister's eyebrow. The community was tightly-knit with neighbors watching out for neighbors and several social and charitable clubs were well established. There was no shortage of dedicated manpower for fire fighting, most being merchants or farmers close enough to make the run into town, all being sturdy enough to manually pull the hose and ladder wagons through the streets.

The flames are leaping aloft in the air, lighting the country with its terrible glare; The sparks by the million, both large and small, are firing the roofs as they continue to fall. Our barns, our stables, and stacks of hay, will soon from us be taken away; They are all now in flames, no use to resist, this terrible fire, they cannot miss.

Written in October 1895 by an unknown author a multi-stanza poem captured the anguish of the Plano community as a disastrous fire swept through the downtown, destroying 51 businesses and several residences. The third such fire to destroy downtown Plano over a 14-year period, the *Great Fire of 1895* provided the impetus to prompt the citizens to petition for the formal organization of the Plano Fire Department, which came to pass in February 1897.

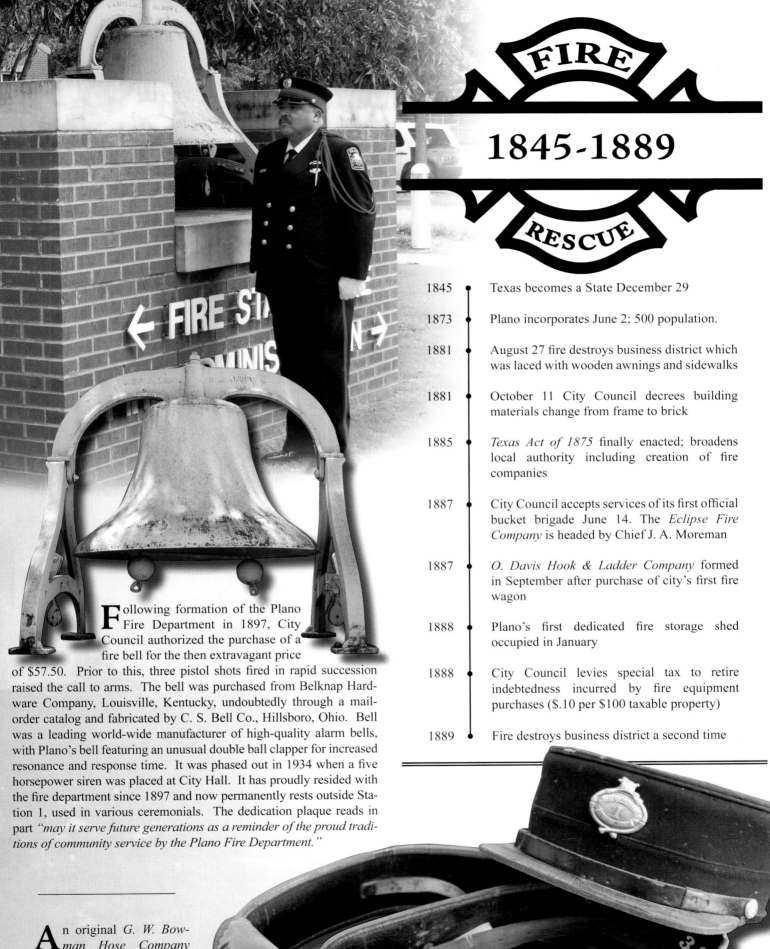

1845	Texas becomes a State December 29
1873	Plano incorporates June 2; 500 population.
1881	August 27 fire destroys business district which was laced with wooden awnings and sidewalks
1881	October 11 City Council decrees building materials change from frame to brick
1885	*Texas Act of 1875* finally enacted; broadens local authority including creation of fire companies
1887	City Council accepts services of its first official bucket brigade June 14. The *Eclipse Fire Company* is headed by Chief J. A. Moreman
1887	*O. Davis Hook & Ladder Company* formed in September after purchase of city's first fire wagon
1888	Plano's first dedicated fire storage shed occupied in January
1888	City Council levies special tax to retire indebtedness incurred by fire equipment purchases ($.10 per $100 taxable property)
1889	Fire destroys business district a second time

Following formation of the Plano Fire Department in 1897, City Council authorized the purchase of a fire bell for the then extravagant price of $57.50. Prior to this, three pistol shots fired in rapid succession raised the call to arms. The bell was purchased from Belknap Hardware Company, Louisville, Kentucky, undoubtedly through a mail-order catalog and fabricated by C. S. Bell Co., Hillsboro, Ohio. Bell was a leading world-wide manufacturer of high-quality alarm bells, with Plano's bell featuring an unusual double ball clapper for increased resonance and response time. It was phased out in 1934 when a five horsepower siren was placed at City Hall. It has proudly resided with the fire department since 1897 and now permanently rests outside Station 1, used in various ceremonials. The dedication plaque reads in part *"may it serve future generations as a reminder of the proud traditions of community service by the Plano Fire Department."*

An original *G. W. Bowman Hose Company* hat and belt, proudly displayed at Fire Administration, Station 1.

FIRE
1890-1899
RESCUE

An 1899 photo of the newly formed *G. W. Bowman Hose Company* at an Independence Day celebration showcasing the team of Dan and Dude who arrived in March of that year. The formation of this company marked the conversion from manually pulled to horse drawn wagons. At far left is E. O. Harrington who would champion the purchase of the department's infamous chemical wagon. Fifth from right is long-time firefighter Gee Hudson who would be voted in as Fire Chief on several occasions.

1890	Plano population estimated between 1,200 – 1,500
1890	30-foot deep well dedicated solely to fire brigades dug downtown September 9
1891	Two-wheel manually pulled hand operated pump and hose cart acquired January 13
1893	Plano Ordinance No. 93 passed in March defining Plano's fire limits and the class of structures allowed therein

1895 Fire

The fires that ravaged Plano's economic center affected the entire region with Plano businessmen the catalyst for the creation of an organized fire department. An 1895 photograph of the Plano School Board and Faculty provides a rare photo of J. A. Moreman (#1) chief of Plano's first organized "fire bucket brigade," the *Eclipse Fire Company*. Also pictured is Olney Davis (#2). His championing for better equipment for the "fire boys" resulted in the 1887 purchase of a hand drawn hook and ladder wagon, organized as the *O. Davis Hook and Ladder Company*. The 1893 purchase of Plano's hand-drawn chemical engine was facilitated by the consistent efforts of S. M. Harrington (#3), resulting in the formation of the *S. M. Harrington Chemical Company*. All worked to improve Plano's fire fighting capabilities, joining voices with other prominent Plano businessmen and landholders.

1895 Fire

1893	*S. M. Harrington Chemical Company* formed with arrival of first chemical engine & 200 feet of hose in November
1894	First City Hall opens in February housing calaboose, fire apparatus storage and livery stable
1894	City Council enacts ordinance prohibiting steam operated corn shellers, mills, cotton gins, threshers or any other steam machinery that might cause fires
1894	At March meeting City Council elects Stopple, Hays, Mathews, Morgan and Kendrick to form the *Plano Fire Company* with John Gates elected Chief
1895	The *Great Fire of 1895* destroys 51 businesses and multiple residences in Plano's most devastating fire
1897	Site location and plans for a dam on Spring Creek to create Plano's first water works are approved by City Council March 9; First water mains authorized shortly thereafter
1897	Citizens petition in February for formation of organized Fire Department after 19 buildings are destroyed in business district fire
1897	City Council meets in May to recognize several citizens as the *Plano Fire Department* appointing Ralph Wyatt Plano's first fire Chief with sleeping quarters provided at City Hall
1897	Fire alarm bell purchased for $57.50 for top of City Hall, replacing pistol shots as fire signal. (Currently rests at Fire Station No. 1)
1897	City Council passes City of Plano Ordinance No. 116 September 14 regulating and governing the Plano Fire Department
1898	At June 14 meeting City Council allots $2.00 per month for two teams to practice twice monthly
1899	In March City Council approves manually drawn hose and chemical wagon conversions to horse drawn. Team of Dan and Dude are purchased; *G. W. Bowman Hose Company* formed

FIRE
1900-1919
RESCUE

1900	Plano population estimated at 1,304
1901	First electric service to Plano lights fire hall sleeping rooms; first telephone installed
1902	George Goode becomes first paid man in department at salary of $5 per month for feeding and care of horses.
1904	Murray "Dag" Hudson hired as first paid on-duty firefighter to live at station, remaining with department until June 1928
1911	Fire destroys *Plano Star Courier* building destroying all Fire Department records housed there
1914	First Plano Fire Department *Constitution & By-laws* approved by City Council March 13
1915	*Big Tom* becomes Plano's first automotive engine. A Thomas Flyer Automobile is converted with a pump and hose bed, purchased through a $350 donation and wagon/team sale
1917	Plano men and boys leave to join armed forces during WWI with department manpower shortage extending through 1919
1917	The horse-drawn engine era ends with purchase of *Old Puss*, a second Thomas Flyer converted into hose and ladder truck, equipped with a chemical tank

Plano's volunteer firemen ranged from merchants to farm hands. As with any small community, ties were close knit with social engagements ranging from church and lodge meetings to department picnics to fishing trips. Pictured on the porch at "City Hall" are firefighters Dag Hudson on mandolin with R. B. Howey on guitar.

A mid-1900's photo of the *G. W. Bowman Hose Company* in front of the livery. The wear on Dude and Dan is beginning to show with the *Plano Star Courier* championing for replacements. "The beautiful blacks have served their day, racing to many a fire on time with their load of human and mechanical protection' but twelve or thirteen years of this work is enough and is showing on the enduring qualities of both horses. Are we willing to help the boys?" A replacement team was purchased with donated funds, though short-lived as the sounds of automobile horns began to fill the air. The beloved Dude and Dan were indeed put out to pasture, living out their lives on a local farm, still trotting along the fence line when the fire bell rang out.

Dag Hudson, the department's first full-time salaried firefighter, is shown outside a rare photo of Plano's first City Hall. Built in 1894 it featured a calaboose, fire equipment storage and a livery. When this photo was taken in 1906 most of the city had already turned out at the Cotton Belt rail depot to view one of the first automobiles being shipped via flatbed into Dallas. By 1909 the City Council had passed an ordinance forbidding autos to travel over seven miles per hour through the city. Eight years later the age of the horse-drawn engine would come to a close.

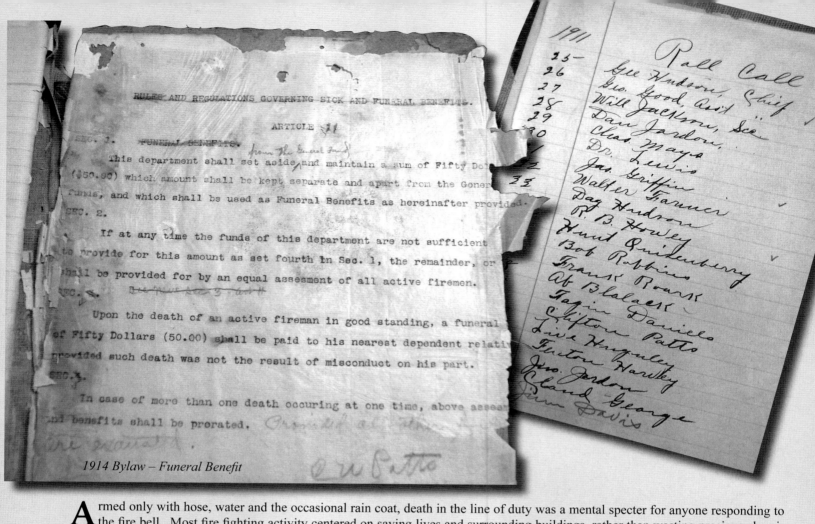

RULES AND REGULATIONS GOVERNING SICK AND FUNERAL BENEFITS.

ARTICLE 1

SEC. 1.   FUNERAL BENEFITS.

from the General Fund

This department shall set aside and maintain a sum of Fifty Dollars ($50.00) which amount shall be kept separate and apart from the General funds, and which shall be used as Funeral Benefits as hereinafter provided.

SEC. 2.

If at any time the funds of this department are not sufficient to provide for this amount as set fourth in Sec. 1, the remainder, or all shall be provided for by an equal assessment of all active firemen.

SEC. 3.

Upon the death of an active fireman in good standing, a funeral of Fifty Dollars (50.00) shall be paid to his nearest dependent relative provided such death was not the result of misconduct on his part.

SEC. 4.

In case of more than one death occuring at one time, above assessment and benefits shall be prorated.

1914 Bylaw – Funeral Benefit

Armed only with hose, water and the occasional rain coat, death in the line of duty was a mental specter for anyone responding to the fire bell. Most fire fighting activity centered on saving lives and surrounding buildings, rather than wasting precious chemicals and water on buildings often long gone by the time the alarm was sounded. This rare 1914 rules and regulations document carefully pasted in a fire minute log states "Upon the death of an active fireman in good standing a funeral of fifty dollars shall be paid to his nearest dependent relative provided such death was not the result of misconduct on his part." In the event funds were not on hand each fireman would be assessed an equal amount. Against all odds, the fifty dollar benefit remained untapped, with the only death to date of an on-duty Plano firefighter occurring in 1950.

This 1905 photo features Dag Hudson at the reins as brother Gee Hudson, often elected Fire Chief by the volunteers, poses in front of the assembly. Volunteers were continually praised for their efforts in putting out fires with one news clipping lauding their efforts stating "the Plano Fire Department cannot be beat when it has an even break."

FIRE
1900-1919
RESCUE

20

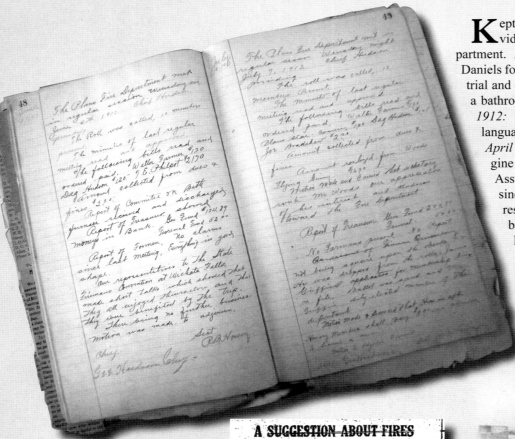

Kept in the City's vaults, handwritten log books provide a fascinating look at the early years of the department. *March 1911:* Charges preferred against fireman Daniels for wearing fireman's hat while off duty. He stood trial and came clear. *March 1912:* Motion carried that a bathroom heater be purchased and installed. *October 1912:* Motion made to fire Jordan for using indecent language but he pled guilty and was fined ten cents. *April 1913:* One line of hose laid and chemical engine used at Huguleys Gin Fire. *September 1913:* Asst. Forman of E&H Company reported two fires since the last meeting with one at Charlie Smith's residence August 26 a total loss on account of bad water pressure. *February 1914:* Fireman Roark let his tongue slip to the tune of 25 cents. Blalack was fined 20 cents for being absent at the last meeting and a 10 cent fine was paid by Huguley for missing roll call. *September 1918:* Motion carried that fireman Shipp, having gone to war, be carried on the non-active list without dues until he returns. *June 1919:* Motion carried that the department buy 12 coats, 12 hats and smoke masks.

PLANO'S FIRST FIRE IN FOUR MONTHS

The Home of J. H. Hutton Total Destroyed Saturday Night.

Saturday night shortly after 8 o'clock the alarm of fire was heard in Plano for the first time in four months and it was soon learned that the house owned by J. H. Hutton, and occupied by himself and family, in the south part of town, was on fire. Owing to the distance from the fire station, it was some time before the fire department could reach the scene, but because of the fact that the water mains do not reach that far, there was little that could be done. The chemical engine was used on the barn, which was pretty close to the house, and it was saved, together with several hundred dollars' worth of lumber which was stored in it.

A SUGGESTION ABOUT FIRES

I kindly ask, in the name of the Plano Fire Department, that useless alarms be not turned in at every occasion of imaginary fire danger. We solicit prompt action when danger exists and pledge prompt response to all calls, but recently the fire department has been several times called out and others disturbed and excited, when the slightest effort would have instantly shown no danger. We want to be called on when needed, but merely suggest that a slight investigation will sometimes save us great effort and expense and the public from annoyance and excitement.

GEE HUDSON, CHIEF
PLANO FIRE DEPARTMENT.

The Fire Department was called out about 3 o'clock last Sunday afternoon by a fire at the Huguley gin in South Plano. A bale of cotton in the press, where the fire originated, was practically destroyed, but the Department succeeded in preventing the further spread of the fire by the use of hand extinguishers and the chemical engine. No water was found necessary.

We should remember that the Fire Department has seldom called upon the people of Plano for help. When they needed coats, hats and boots it was from their funds, donated them, that they were bought. Some of the nozzles, wrenches and a part of the other equipment were in bad condition and from their own funds this was added. The alarm system was bad, and from the same financial source the money came to buy and equip a motor alarm, which is as good as any in the country. It is often the case that fighting a fire is very dirty work, and a bath room was needed. The money for this came also from their own funds.

By-Laws of the Plano Fire Department 18

Bath Tub Rules and Regulations.

Rule 1. No person shall be allowed the use of bath tub or room unless he be a member of this Department, or some other fire company of this State, in good standing.

Rule 2. Any person or persons violating Rule 1, is trespassing and shall be dealt with accordingly.

Rule 3. No member or members shall have the right to permit any person the use of tub or room, unless such person shall be eligible as per Rule 1.

Rule 4. It shall be the duty of each member to report at the next regular meeting any violation of Rule 1 or 3, which he may know to have occurred and any member failing to comply with this Rule, i. e., Rule 4, shall be fined not less than $1.00 for each offense, and shall be expelled from the Department, if such fine is not paid by the next regular meeting.

Rule 5. Whenever a complaint is made as per Rule 4, it shall be the duty of the presiding officer to appoint a committee of three which shall include the person or persons making such complaint, and it shall be the duty of this committee to investigate such charges and render a verdict at the next regular meeting.

By-Laws of the Plano Fire Department 19

Rule. 6. Any member violating Rule 3, shall be fined not less than $1.00 for each offense, such fine to be paid by the next regular meeting after verdict is rendered; otherwise the member shall be suspended.

Rule 7. Each member upon using tub shall thoroughly cleanse and rinse tub, floor and walls from any dirt or water resulting from said use and any member violating this Rule shall be fined for the first offense a sum of $1.00; for a second offense shall be denied the use of tub for a period of six months directly following, and for the third offense shall be expelled from the Department.

Rule 8. Each member shall be responsible for any damage to bath room or co... which may happen during his use, or... may be caused by any carelessness or... ligence during his use of room, a... have same repaired to the ... damage within a reasonable... atly following.

Rule 9. Each member ... maintain a private box, ... said bath room, for the ... clothes, towels, etc., pro... shall be fixed and perma... further that said positio... with any of the fixtures... that may be retained ...

STAR-COURIER PLANT IS DESTROYED.
Entire Plant is Destroyed by the Flames at An Early Hour on the Morning of Wednesday, January 4th. ...

THREATENING ...RES AT PLANO
...cox Old Home is Partly Burned—and a School Building Damaged.

BIG COTTON GIN PLANT BURNED FRIDAY NIGHT
The Origin of the Fire is Unknown—the Property Owned in Ft. Worth.

The cotton gin plant of the Fort Worth Cotton Oil Mill located on West Mechanic st...

PLANO FLOUR MILL DESTROYED BY FIRE
Ice Plant and Office Saved by Heroic Ef... forts of Fire Boys—Caught in Elevator Shaft.

Plano Has $35,000.00 Fire Insurance Covering $12,000.00

Origin Not Deffinitely Known—Caught Early in Morning— Populace Awakened by North-Bound Freight Train

Monday morning of this week the three brick buildings owned by J. P. Spillman, on the north side of Mechanic Street, and their contents were destroyed by fire. The cause of the fire is unknown, but it either caught in the rear end of Bert Harmer's restaurant or the tailor shop of Ben Garrett. The fire was first discovered by a northbound freight train which was some distance from the city. As soon as the train rolled into the city it gave some very shrill whistles that brought the populace of the city from their peaceful repose to realization that there was something dreadfully wrong in the city. At about this time the fire bell tolled out the ...lligence that there was a fire in town. The fire was found doing its destructive ... very rapid rate when the fire boys arrived on the scene. The heroes of m... ...st did some of the most valiant service ever done in the history of thi... ...tire town from going up in smoke.

ENORMOUS L...
The losses are very heavy. Some of th... ...thers carried very small amounts. The los... ...an, three two-story brick ...

THANKS TO CITIZENS FROM THE FIRE BOYS

We wish to thank each citizen whose name appears below for the amount opposite their name, which was a free-will gift to us for services rendered at Monday morning's fire.

We are volunteers and we gladly lay aside business and fight your fires and try to save your property, and we can not find words with which to thank you. Our motto is "When Duty Calls 'Tis Ours to Obey." We thank you.

W. C. Armstrong	$ 2.50
A. G. Hays	
Dr. W. D. Ellis	5.00
S. J. Mathews	
W. R. George	10.00
Olney Davis	10.00
I. O. O. F. Lodge	15.00
D. C. George	15.00
Allen Bros.	20.00
Plano National Bank	25.00
	25.00

Yours to serve,
PLANO F... ...PARTMENT.

On March 13, 1914 the first *Constitution and Bylaws* of the Plano Fire Department were passed and approved by City Council. Filled with serious governance policy, the inclusion of rules governing a bath tub may appear out of place. With indoor plumbing facilities still scarce in the 1900's the installation of a bath facility at City Hall was a major event, regularly mentioned in the recorded fire minutes. Committees were continually formed to investigate everything from piping installation and appropriate window coverings. The minutes of October 1, 1913, show a committee tasked to purchase and replace a cut-off valve to the tub and to purchase and install a mirror, shelf and drawer for the facility along with discussion on stricter rules to govern its use. Fines up to one dollar were often levied for improper use of the facility by the volunteers. Following official adoption of the Bylaws sides were chosen as the department investigated the veracity of one firefighter who accused another of leaving a soiled tub with towels on the floor. The accused was eventually found innocent with the accuser leaving the department after paying a hefty fine of $2.50 for false witness.

October 1915 Minutes: Mayor Cottrell and Fire Marshal Wilson together slipped over to the school building, had the fire gong sounded and stood by to observe the results. The mayor says there was no running, no falling down and that the house was vacated with quiet, orderly discipline in one minute and ten seconds. *November 1915:* The department contracted last Monday with the Whitney Show Company. It is said to belong to the better class of street shows playing only important cities like McKinney, Plano and Texarkana. The tents will be reared on Mechanic Street at Main occupying spaces for five shows and fifteen concessions. *December 1915:* The department received from the Whitney Show company last Saturday $43.50, the percentage of receipts of the carnival last week to which we were entitled

The purchase of *Big Tom*, Plano's first automotive engine, may have been the impetus for this wonderful photo. Looking more like members of a country club preparing for a yacht regatta, the fire department gathered for an impromptu portrait in 1915. The ever present Dag Hudson is now at the wheel rather than at the reins. Holding the nozzle is George Goode, who was the first salaried employee of the department, paid $5 for the feeding and care of the horses and excused from street repair duty for a year. It would be up to the skill of the volunteers to maintain the engine and to purchase supplies and parts through fundraisers.

The January 4, 1911, fire at the *Star-Courier* destroyed all records to date of the department. Their elected secretary had taken photos and other materials and stored them in the building, which was considered fire proof. Even the newspaper expressed its surprise stating, "Owing to the fact that this was supposed to be a fire-proof building, the location of the fire was a surprise, not only to us, but to everyone in Plano."

STAR-COURIER PLANT IS DESTROYED.

tire Plant is Destroyed by the Flames at An Early Hour on the Morning of Wednesday, January 4th. —1911

About 3 o'clock Wednesday morning, Jan. 4th, the alarm of fire was sounded in Plano and investigation showed that the office of the Star-Courier was in flames from the front to the rear of the building. Owing to the fact that this was supposed to be a fire-proof building, the location of the fire was a surprise, not only to us, but to everyone in Plano. The fire is bound to have originated in the roof, or rather between the ceiling and the roof, as this was practically the only inflammable part of the building. At the time of its discovery the fire had made such headway that the Fire Department, although it did all that any Department could have done, could not possibly save any of the plant, and all that they could do was to confine the flames to the building in which they originated. This they did, and their success in this instance is but another evidence of what we have always said, that the Plano Fire Department cannot be beat when it has an even break.

It would be useless for us to go into a detailed statment regarding the fire; suffice it to say that it has left us just about where we were when we came to Plano. Since taking charge of the Star-Courier we had paid $1,000.00 of the agreed purchase price. The balance was in notes, and the main object of the insurance which we carried was to protect the holder of these notes, and it was of little pecuniary benefit to us. When summed up, we find that we have lost between $1,000.00 and $1,200.

With a heart overflowing with gratitude to the many friends who have assured us of their sympathy and offered words of encouragement, we present to your charitable consideration the first issue of the rejuvinated Star-Courier, and we extend to every friend of the paper a cordial invitation to come in and inspect our new office. When our big press gets here, in the course of a week or ten days, we will have one of the most complete and up-to-date printing plants in Collin county—or anywhere else.

NEW RUBBER SUITS.   J. S. Dickerson   1.00   E. O. Harrington & Co.

![FIRE 1920-1929 RESCUE logo]

FIRE 1920-1929 RESCUE

1923 • Upon recommendation of Fire Department Committee a new two-story all-brick fire station, City Hall and jail is built with furnishings for $10,672, serving the community until 1966

1925 • Citizens approve bond funding for paving of several Plano streets improving fire response time

1925 • City Hall Fire Bell and hand-operated siren replaced with electric sirens located in top windows of City Hall facing east and west

1927 • Gas installed in Plano, reducing fire risks

1929 • Plano's first false fire alarm recorded June 15

1929 • First factory built truck purchased from Peter Pirsch & Sons for $7,000; retired July 1971, restored and proudly used in ceremonials today

Members of the fire department assembled for an official portrait in 1920. Unpaid, they relied on their own skills to maintain and replace equipment, and upon their own creativity to organize fundraisers to purchase everything from rain coats to hose to tires for the vehicles. They learned the skills of the trade by the seat of their pants with an occasional training session offered by firefighters from other cities. They sported broken arms, sprained ankles, bruises and burns and willingly came back for more. An integral part of the department, seldom identified in photos, was the Chaplain, who regularly attended meetings and social functions, offering words of encouragement and the power of faith. Pictured are *Front Row:* Bob Howery, C. Klepper. *Second Row:* Gee Hudson, G. Goode, B. Klepper, T. O. Ray. *Third Row:* H. Barkham, S. Blanke, Bert Sherrill, Dag Hudson, C. Mayes, W. Muggar.

Realizing the need to modernize their equipment, the fire department went before City Council in 1915 offering to donate $350 toward an auto fire truck if the council would approve the sale of one team of horses and a wagon to complete the purchase. A Thomas Flyer automobile, immediately nicknamed *Big Tom*, soon arrived with the firemen and citizens using their skills to build their first fire truck. "The truck arrived in Plano last Saturday and is in the garage waiting to be converted into a modern fire fighting machine! This is a great advancement that the fire fighters of Plano have made and the business men and citizens of the city are showing their appreciation by donating to same" proclaimed the *Plano Star Courier* in April 1915.

By November 1915 funds were still being solicited, "We want to say there remains $250 to be paid on the fire truck. It has cost us perhaps a little over $1,500 and it's a fine one, answering every purpose after rigid test…Be it great or small we will appreciate any subscription from anyone who thinks our company is useful to them." Following a fundraising carnival the big day arrived with the *Plano Star Courier* proclaiming on December 10, 1915: "The new fire truck will be brought out for a final demonstration next Monday, Tradesday, at 2 pm. The demonstration will be at the junction of Main and East Mechanic Streets at the post office corner and afterwards the truck will be installed at the fire station ready for service."

The remaining team of horses and wagon worked alongside Big Tom until 1917, when a second Thomas Flyer was purchased and retrofit. The debut of Old Puss marked the end of the horse-drawn fire service era in Plano. *Big Tom* and *Old Puss* remained in service until 1930 when local mechanics combined parts from the two engines to deck out a new engine, rumored to have been a Sears delivery truck.

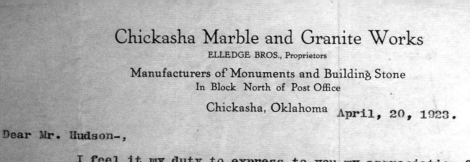

Chickasha Marble and Granite Works

ELLEDGE BROS., Proprietors

Manufacturers of Monuments and Building Stone
In Block North of Post Office

Chickasha, Oklahoma   April, 20, 1923.

Dear Mr. Hudson-,

I feel it my duty to express to you my appreciation for the kindness you and the Plano Fire Department extended my dear mother during her life. I wish to acknowlege my sincerity to each and every one of you for your courtesy toward her. She always talked of the kindness of the Department, and each Christmas she valued very highly the gift she always recieved from you. Her one desire was to someday repay you men.

If ever I can be of service to you in anyway whatever, I will gladly respond to your call. I consider the most I can do, would never repay any kindness ever offered my dear mother.

Sincerely yours –

C. B. (Buckham) Cline
Chickasha, Okla.

The "fire boys" proudly pose in front of the old City Hall with their portly fire dog. This photo was taken after the 1929 arrival of the new Pirsch engine and is probably the last photo of *Old Puss,* who would be used as scrap in the early 1930's to retrofit the Sears delivery truck, along with parts from *Big Tom.*

Plano Texas Jan 7° 1926

Plano Fire Dpt.
            Gentlemen.
            I hereby make application for
membership to your Department, and if elected, [promise]
to make you good Fireman.
            Yours Very Truly.

A. Waits
R. McFarlin
Day Hudson
Earl Waits

FIRE
1920-1929
RESCUE

On Friday, October 25, 1929, the Plano Fire Department took its brand new Peter Pirsch fire truck out for a trial spin, formally accepting receipt the next day to the applause and cheers of the gathered crowd. The Peter Pirsch and Sons Company, Kenosha, Wisconsin, had just delivered Plano's first factory-built engine. It was hot off the assembly line, gleaming red in the sunlight with golden glints bouncing from brass fittings. No longer would volunteer firefighters have to improvise engines from salvaged apparatus, welding bits and pieces from various vehicles onto a recycled chassis.

With the purchase of the Pirsch, Plano became the first town in Collin County to motorize its fire department. The "Pirsch Champion" was purchased with a 600-gallon pumper and a few other special options; a one quart CTC fire extinguisher for $8, two extra electric hand lanterns for $24 and a locomotive type fire bell for $36.

The invoice price for the 1929 fire truck is listed at $8,000 but the paperwork shows a $1,000 "allowance for an old combination car" bringing the price for the engine to $7,000.

The Pirsch remains a treasured symbol of Plano's first major leap into the 20th century. The City had committed an unheard sum to support the efforts of the Plano Fire Department and the investment paid off. The Pirsch remained in active duty until the 1970s, helping to save countless lives and returning hundreds of thousands of dollars to the community in saved real estate.

After being retired from service, students from the Plano High School auto body class worked alongside firefighters for a complete restoration of the truck. Today it can still be seen in parades and at special events, a proud legacy of our fire suppression past.

FIRE

1920-1929

RESCUE

PLANO FIRE DEPT.

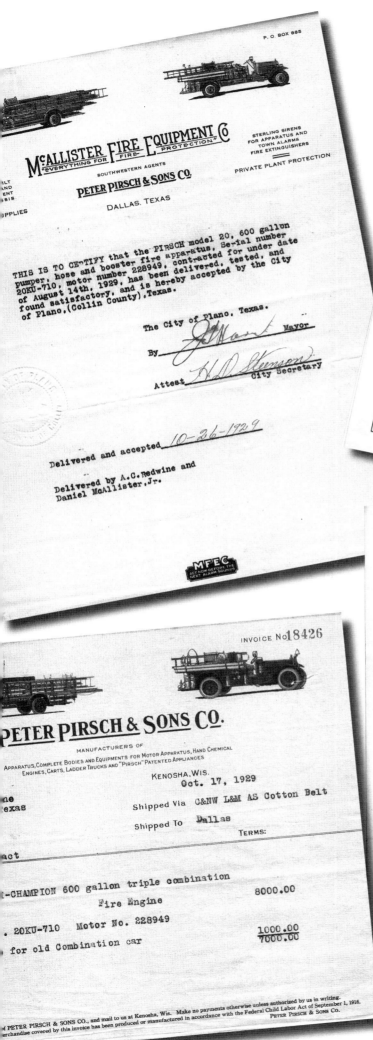

P. O. BOX 885

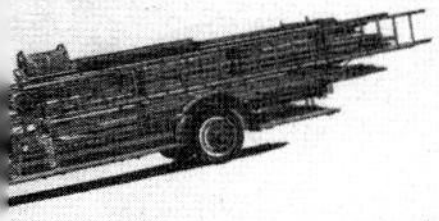

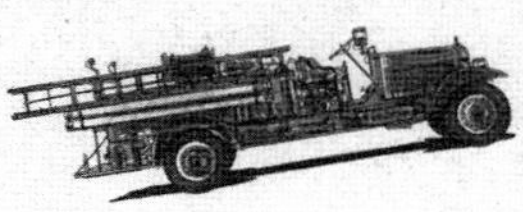

McALLISTER FIRE EQUIPMENT Co
"EVERYTHING FOR FIRE PROTECTION"

...ILT
...AND
...ENT
...SSIS

...PPLIES

STERLING SIRENS FOR APPARATUS AND TOWN ALARMS
FIRE EXTINGUISHERS

PRIVATE PLANT PROTECTION

SOUTHWESTERN AGENTS
PETER PIRSCH & SONS CO.
DALLAS, TEXAS

THIS IS TO CERTIFY that the PIRSCH model 20, 600 gallon pumper, hose and booster fire apparatus, Serial number 20KU-710, motor number 228949, contracted for under date of August 14th, 1929, has been delivered, tested, and found satisfactory, and is hereby accepted by the City of Plano, (Collin County), Texas.

The City of Plano, Texas.

By *[signature]* Mayor

Attest *H. D. Stevenson* City Secretary

Delivered and accepted *10-26-1929*

Delivered by A.C.Redwine and Daniel McAllister,Jr.

MFEC
ACT NOW BEFORE THE NEXT ALARM SOUNDS

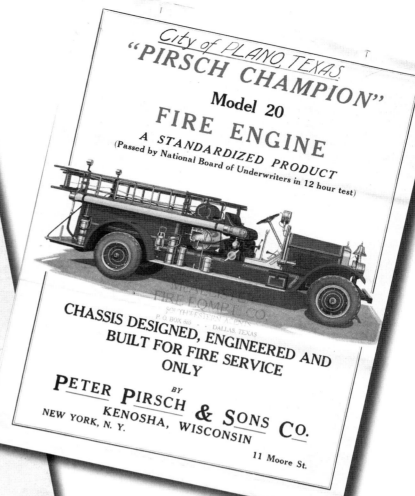

City of PLANO, TEXAS.

"PIRSCH CHAMPION"

Model 20

FIRE ENGINE

A STANDARDIZED PRODUCT
(Passed by National Board of Underwriters in 12 hour test)

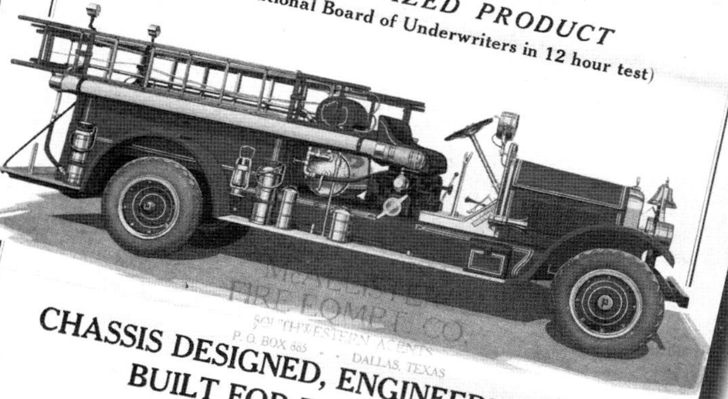

McALLISTER FIRE EQUIPMENT CO.
SOUTHWESTERN AGENTS
P. O. BOX 885
DALLAS, TEXAS

CHASSIS DESIGNED, ENGINEERED AND BUILT FOR FIRE SERVICE ONLY

BY

PETER PIRSCH & SONS CO.
KENOSHA, WISCONSIN

NEW YORK, N. Y.
11 Moore St.

INVOICE No 18426

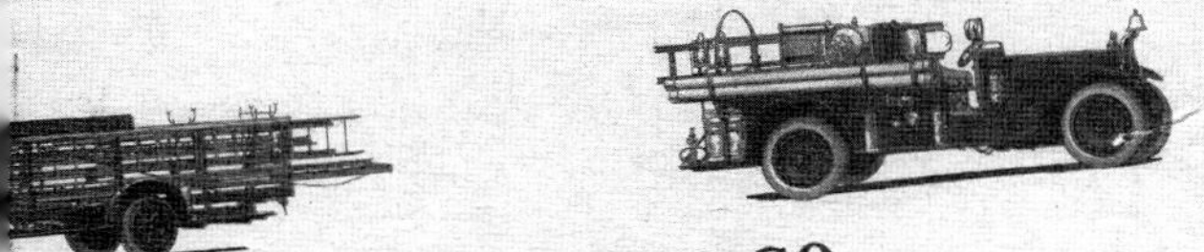

PETER PIRSCH & SONS CO.

MANUFACTURERS OF
...APPARATUS, COMPLETE BODIES AND EQUIPMENTS FOR MOTOR APPARATUS, HAND CHEMICAL ENGINES, CARTS, LADDER TRUCKS AND "PIRSCH" PATENTED APPLIANCES

KENOSHA, WIS.
Oct. 17, 1929

...ne
...exas

Shipped Via C&NW L&M AS Cotton Belt

Shipped To Dallas

TERMS:

...act

...-CHAMPION 600 gallon triple combination Fire Engine	8000.00
... 20KU-710 Motor No. 228949	
... for old Combination car	1000.00
	7000.00

...of PETER PIRSCH & SONS CO., and mail to us at Kenosha, Wis. Make no payments otherwise unless authorized by us in writing.
...erchandise covered by this invoice has been produced or manufactured in accordance with the Federal Child Labor Act of September 1, 1916.
PETER PIRSCH & SONS CO.

PETER PIRSCH & SONS CO.

Waukasha CHASSIS—*Specifications*

MOTOR—~~80~~ *87* Hose Power, Six cylinder, Fire Apparatus Motor.

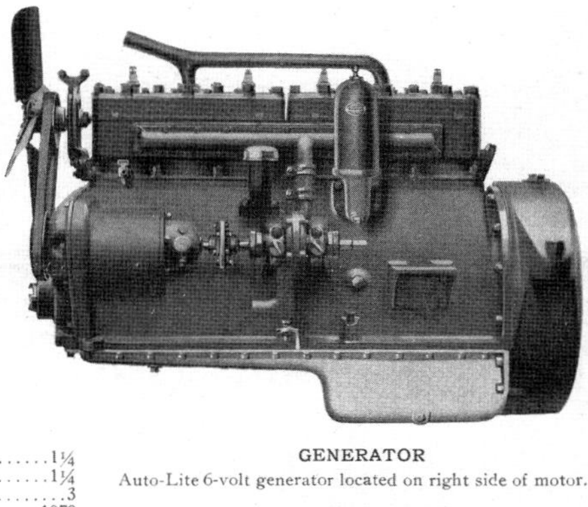

MOTOR DIMENSIONS—

Bore	4
Stroke	4¾
Displacement	358
Valve diameter, clear	1¾
Connecting rod bearing	2¾ x 1½
Front main bearing	3 x 1⅞
First intermediate bearing	3 x 1½
Second intermediate bearing	3 x 1½
Third intermediate bearing	3 x 3
Fourth intermediate bearing	3 x 1½
Fifth intermediate bearing	3 x 1½
Rear main bearing	3 x 3
Piston pin bearing	1 x 2
Connecting rod—ct. to ct.	10¼
Camshaft diameter	1⅜
Timing gears—face	1½
Piston rings—number	3
Piston rings—width	$\frac{3}{16}$
Spark plugs—S.A.E.	⅞ x 18
Carburetor flange—S.A.E.	1½
Exhaust manifold—bore	2½
Fan diameter	18
Water inlet	1¼
Water outlet	1¼
Flywheel housing—S.A.E., No.	3
Weight	1070

NOTE — All dimensions are given in inches.

EQUIPMENT AND MATERIAL—

Crankshaft—S.A.E. 1045 steel, heat treated.
Crankcase—Cast Iron-Exceptionally deep "Girder Type."
Connecting Rods—S.A.E. 1045 steel, heat treated. Bearings cast directly into big ends.
Main Bearings—Bronze back with Fahrig metal lining.
Valves—Special alloy with flat case-hardened end.
Push Rods—⅝-inch diameter, hollow, case-hardened, and ground; mushroom type, lock nut adjustment.
Cylinders—Ricardo split head design. Chrome nickel iron, bored and ground to close limits.
Cylinder Heads—Ricardo patent design.
Timing Gears—Semi-steel and steel, very wide.
Cooling System—Rugged centrifugal pump.
Lubrication—Force-feed to main, connecting rod and camshaft bearings and idler stud.

CARBURETOR—

Stromberg vertical float level type which provides uniform mixture at all motor speeds; size 1½-inch S.A.E.

FUEL SYSTEM—

Large gasoline tank of heavy steel with large inlet. Fuel is fed by means of gravity through strainer and best armored flexible gasoline line of ample size.

IGNITION

Robert Bosch Auto-Lite dual system is supplied. Battery and high tension magneto. Two separate sets of spark plugs; each set can be operated separately or simultaneously from switch on dash.

GENERATOR

Auto-Lite 6-volt generator located on right side of motor.

STARTING MOTOR

Auto-Lite 6-volt with double X Bendix drive. Starting switch located on floor board. Hand starting crank is also provided.

CLUTCH

Multiple dry disc of ample size for torque of motor. Long life is obtained primarily by the large amount of bearing surface on the several discs. An extra heavy spring insures positive contact; all steel plates are hardened and ground and the best quality disc facing is used.

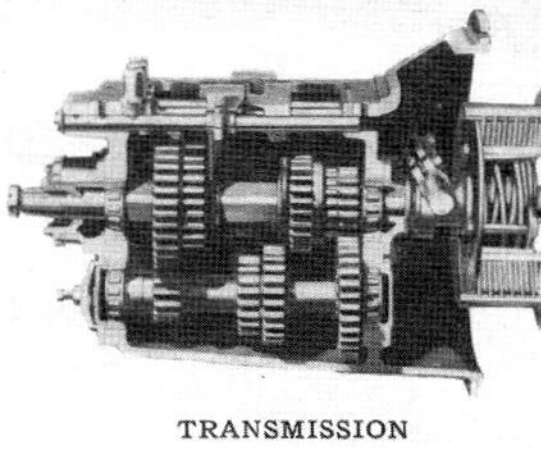

TRANSMISSION

Four speeds forward and one reverse selective sliding gear unit with motor. All gears and shafts are made of the best alloy steel properly hardened and ground. Bearings are of the anti-friction type.

Page 3

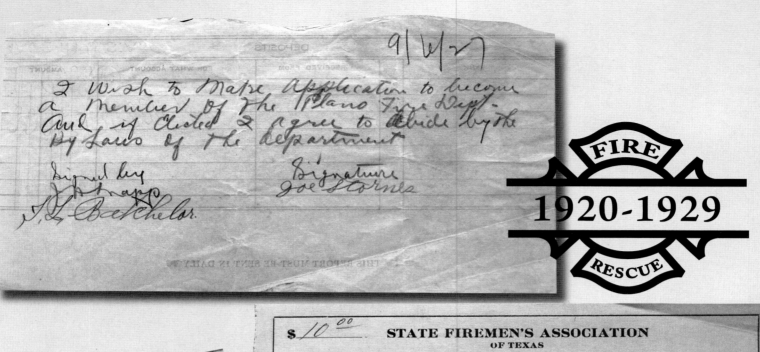

9/6/27

I Wish to Make Application to become
a Member Of the Plano Fire Dept.
And if Elected I agree to Abide by the
By Laws of the Department.

Signed by   Signature
J. A. Rapp   Joe Stormes
S. L. Batchelor.

FIRE
1920-1929
RESCUE

NEW RUBBER SUITS.

The following is a list of those who contributed to the purchase of new rubber suits for the Plano Fire Department. These suits were badly needed and the Department is appreciative of the spirit which prompted their purchase:

& M. Bank _____	$ 5.00 One Suit
H. Gulledge _____	8.00
Plano Nat'l Bank _____	2.50
M. C. Portman _____	2.00
D. C. George _____	2.00
I. W. Hays _____	2.50
Allen Brothers _____	1.00
M. Forman _____	1.00
& A. Carpenter _____	
First Guaranty State Bank	4.00

$ 10⁰⁰   STATE FIREMEN'S ASSOCIATION
OF TEXAS
OFFICE OF RECORDING SECRETARY
3-17   1928
Received of Plano Fire Dept
Ten and 00/100   Dollars
Dues for 1928
                              STATE FIREMEN'S ASSOCIATION OF TEXAS
①
Per _____ Rec. Sect'y.

1928 Fire Association Receipt.

NO. ____   Treasury Warrant.
To the Depository of the Plano Fire Department, Plano, Texas:
Pay to D. g. Hudson   or order $ 2 25
Two and 50/100   DOLLARS
out of GENERAL FUND for _____
By the order of the Fire Department. Witness our hand this 7 day of Feb 192
G. H. Hudson ____ CHIEF.   GENERAL FUND.
C. N. Potts ____ SECRETARY.   ____ TREASURER.

Plano, Texas.
August 9th, 1930.

Mr. A. L. Merritt,
Plano, Texas.

Dear Mr. Merritt:

At the last regular meeting of the Plano Fire Department, on motion, the secretary was instructed to write you expressing the thanks and appreciation of the Department for your generous remembrance of its organization.

Expressions of this kind and recognition of our neighbors and fellow citizens of the service that we are trying to render this community unselfishly and to the best of our ability, gives a great deal of encouragement to the Department, and it is with the most sincere thanks and gratitude that we write you.

Very sincerely yours,

Secretary,

PLANO FIRE DEPARTMENT.

ONH::RC.
CC   G. E. Carpenter.
      Mrs. Emma Bishop.
      Mrs. Nannie Bishop.

Then as now, drills enhanced teamwork, performance and response time. Competitions were held throughout the region resulting in friendly rivalries which spurred on greater training and enthusiasm through the year. Plano volunteers were tough competitors in local competitions bringing home over the years everything from bowling trophies to rodeo belts. These trophies recognized the Plano team for excellence proclaiming "Award to Progressive Volunteer Fireman's Association, Competitive Engine Drill, Plano, Texas, 8-13-35, 5-12-36."

1930   Plano population: 1,554

1930   Converted Sears delivery truck with parts from *Big Tom* and *Old Puss* combine with Pirsch to provide total pumping capacity of 1,100 gpm

1930   Volunteer department numbers grow to 21 members

1934   Fire Department begins to police grounds at football games

1936   Reverend W. T. Thurman was nominated as Chaplain and asked to serve the department "as such the remainder of his life"

1939   Department purchases set of wire cutters to carry on truck so electric wires running into buildings may be cut

FIRE
1930-1939
RESCUE

Alarms – 1933

Special Funds

2	Griffin Jim
3	Higuley L. A.
4	Good Geo
5	Standefer Jim
6	Dean John
7	Hotel Earl
8	Batchelor T. L.
9	Coffey E. P.
10	Heilgicor Phil
11	Hughston O. N.
12	Haynes Joe
13	Stogner Sam
14	Wyatt George
15	Yarbrough Ray
16	Stenson Harry
17	Hays James
18	Harrington Jack
19	Eads Lenard
20	Mathews C. J.
21	Tuzzell Geo

1938 Plano Presbyterian Church Fire

32

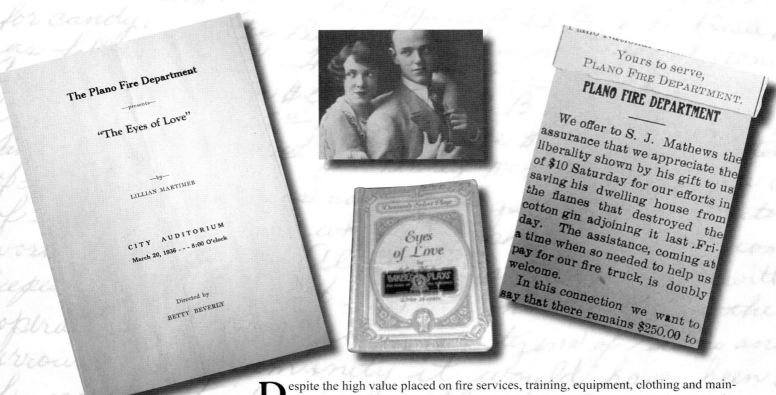

The Plano Fire Department

— presents —

"The Eyes of Love"

— by —

LILLIAN MARTIMER

CITY AUDITORIUM

March 20, 1936 · · · 8:00 O'clock

Directed by

BETTY BEVERLY

Eyes of Love by

Yours to serve,
PLANO FIRE DEPARTMENT.

PLANO FIRE DEPARTMENT

We offer to S. J. Mathews the assurance that we appreciate the liberality shown by his gift to us of $10 Saturday for our efforts in saving his dwelling house from the flames that destroyed the cotton gin adjoining it last Friday. The assistance, coming at a time when so needed to help us pay for our fire truck, is doubly welcome.

In this connection we want to say that there remains $250.00 to

Despite the high value placed on fire services, training, equipment, clothing and maintenance of engines were primarily funded from donations raised through community dinners, plays, raffles and picnics. This was no easy feat as Plano joined the nation in recovering from the Great Depression during the early 1930's. The department relied heavily on donations from those businesses and residents who had benefited from their services, with a voluntary cash donation normally handed over by a grateful property owner after a fire call had been answered. Lillian Martimer's nationally-known three-act comedy The Eyes of Love was a successful fundraiser whose simple but entertaining scripting allowed it to be easily presented by amateur theatre companies. Performed at Plano's 'City Auditorium' it no doubt played before a packed audience, eager for the chance at a night of laughter, supporting a worthy cause.

FIRE

1930-1939

RESCUE

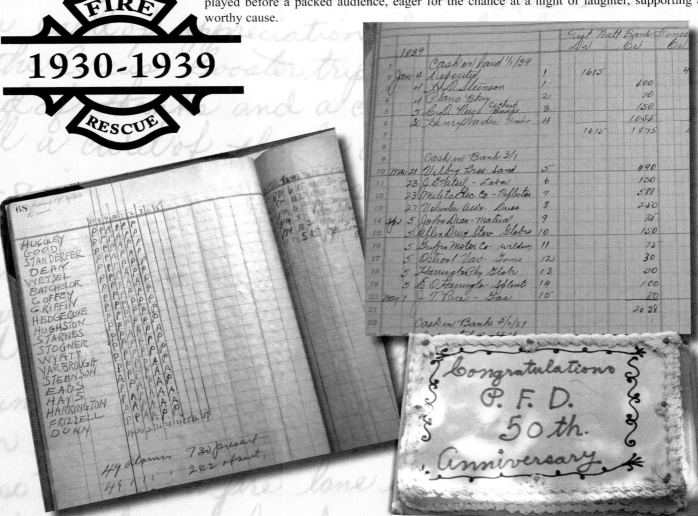

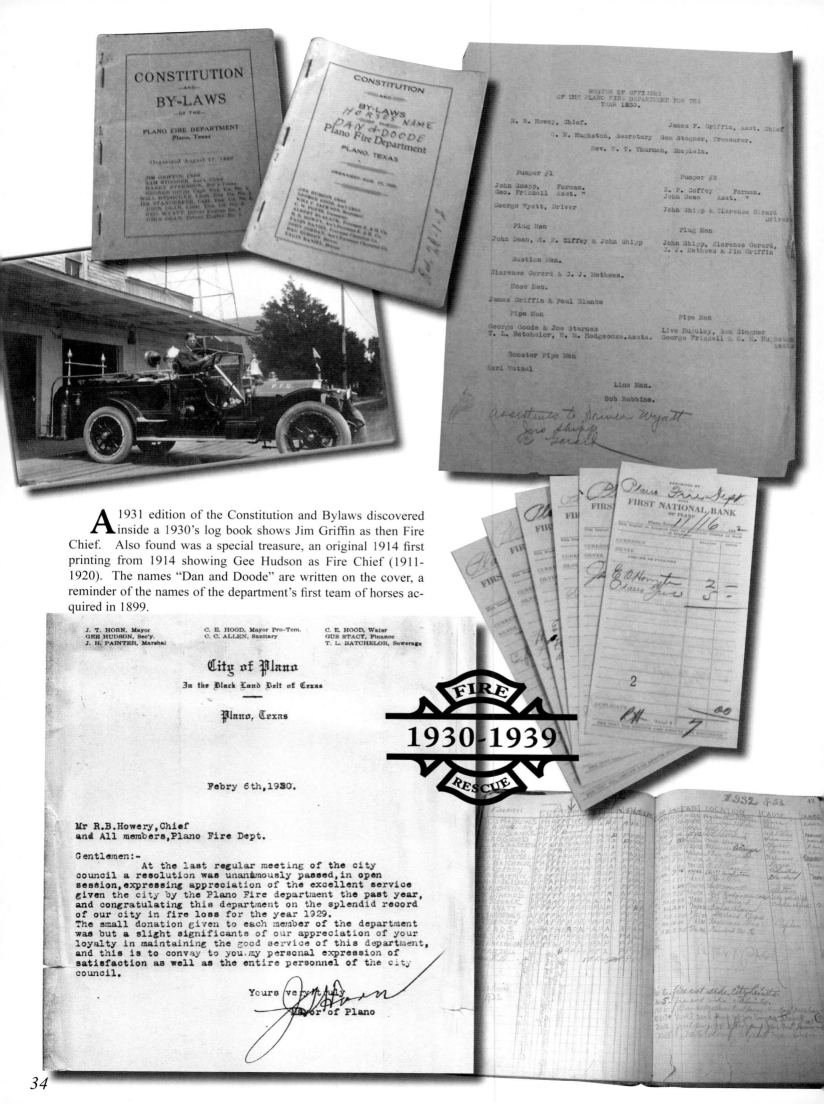

A 1931 edition of the Constitution and Bylaws discovered inside a 1930's log book shows Jim Griffin as then Fire Chief. Also found was a special treasure, an original 1914 first printing from 1914 showing Gee Hudson as Fire Chief (1911-1920). The names "Dan and Doode" are written on the cover, a reminder of the names of the department's first team of horses acquired in 1899.

FIRE
1930-1939
RESCUE

J. T. HORN, Mayor
GEE HUDSON, Sec'y.
J. H. PAINTER, Marshal

C. E. HOOD, Mayor Pro-Tem.
C. C. ALLEN, Sanitary

C. E. HOOD, Water
GUS STACY, Finance
T. L. BATCHELOR, Sewerage

City of Plano

In the Black Land Belt of Texas

Plano, Texas

Febry 6th, 1930.

Mr R.B.Howery,Chief
and All members,Plano Fire Dept.

Gentlemen:-
At the last regular meeting of the city council a resolution was unanimously passed,in open session,expressing appreciation of the excellent service given the city by the Plano Fire department the past year, and congratulating this department on the splendid record of our city in fire loss for the year 1929.
The small donation given to each member of the department was but a slight significants of our appreciation of your loyalty in maintaining the good service of this department, and this is to convay to you my personal expression of satisfaction as well as the entire personnel of the city council.

Yours very truly
Mayor of Plano

FIRE
1940-1949
RESCUE

1940 • Plano population: 1,582

1940 • Volunteers resort to hosting circus events and numerous mountain oyster fry and barbecue dinners to raise funds for departmental equipment and vehicles

1941 • The *Constitution and Bylaws* were amended requiring membership in the Fireman Pension system

1942 • A stopwatch was purchased to aid in training drills

1945 • Department purchases first closed cab fire truck, a 1942 Army surplus 500-gallon Dodge fire truck

1947 • Department raises $1,200 for purchase of iron lung for use on polio cases

1947 • Department membership numbers 25 volunteer firefighters

1947 • 58th Anniversary of the PFD was held with a station Open House demonstrating fire equipment, followed by refreshments for over 150 attendees

1948 • Gainesville Circus event raises funds for uniforms and purchase of 1946 Ford panel truck equipped with 250-watt power plant

1949 • Plano records 55 fire plugs

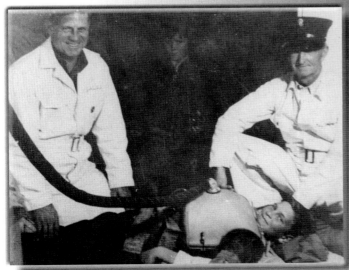

This 1947 photo shows long-time Fire Chief John Dean responding to a fire alarm. Most volunteers had their gear at the ready at both home and the workplace, rushing to answer an alarm with little or no hesitation. By 1949 the department boasted twenty-five volunteers, one paid fireman, three trucks and first-aid emergency equipment, including an iron lung.

ROSTER

PLANO FIRE DEPARTMENT

J. H. Standerfer	Chief
J. W. Hays	Asst. Chief
Raymond Dupree	Capt. No. 1
Harold Garrett	Capt. No. 2
Homer Horton	Lieut. No. 1
C. C. Oliver	Lieut. No. 2

Harold Garrett
John Dean } Instructors

Anderson, Benton
Hinton, Raymond
Horton, B. J.
Jinks, Jno.
Landers, Cletis
Landers, Cylde
Morgan, Roy Sr.
Morgan, Roy Jr.
Painter, Chas.
Randles, E. A.
Sheridan, Dick
Swindle, Bob
Smith, W. W. Sr.
Smith, W. W. Jr.
Todd, Clyde
Todd, James
Todd, Odise
Yarbrough, Ray

Regular Meetings - 1948 -

PLUG LOCATIONS   PLANO, TEXAS

AVE.	ST.	ST.	AVE
K—10th	Braindine	18th	H Bowes
K—1200 Blk	Tripp & Davis	18th	I Carpenter
K—1300 Blk		17th	H
*K—14th	Deany Sinclar	16th	G Johnson
*K—15th (S)	Harrington F.	16th	800 Blk Haggard
*K—15th (N)	Shaw	16th	H School
*K—15th PL	Christies	16th	J Hart
K—16th	M Church	15th	F Hinton
K—1700 Blk	Mitchell	15th	G Funeral H.
K—18th PL	Salmons	15th	Hie Church
L—11th	Hartline	*15th	J Bank
L—12th PL	Lankford	*15th	S. M. H. Arrington
Farmers Gin		14th	F Daniel
L—14th	Howey	14th	G (N) Dunn
*City Hall		14th	G (S)
L—16th		14th	I
M—14th	Batchlor		
M—15th	Pierce		3 ADKINS W. HSE.
M—16th		13th	G PL
N—14th		13th	H PL
N—15th		13th	I
N—15th PL		12th	I
O—15th			
*1600 Blk 15th PL		H. ANGEL	
1600 Klk 15th			
1500 Blk 14th		*Plugs With	
*P—14th	Bay	Steamer Conn.	
*SURE HEAT			
*J—14th	Ice House		
J—1300 Blk			
J—12th PL			

Certificate of Membership
PLANO FIRE DEPARTMENT

Plano, Texas Dec 8 19 1949

To Mr. Scott Bell

At a regular meeting of Plano Fire Department held on Dec 6-19-49 you were duly elected a member. I beg to direct your attention to the annexed copy of Constitution and By-Laws.

Respectfully
W. W. Smith
Secy.-Treas.

FIRE
1940-1949
RESCUE

Did you see the baby in the window below? It was back in 1901 when sleeping quarters were installed inside City Hall for the convenience of the exhausted firemen returning from a fire. When the new Central Fire Station/City Hall was constructed in 1923 family living quarters were added. A full-time fireman was stationed at the facility to sound the alarm, answer telephones and provide a fire presence for anyone in need. At least two fire families resided in city hall including that of Willie Washington Smith. It is undoubtedly one of the Smith twins pictured in the window. The practice was discontinued in 1966 when the new Central Fire Station/City Hall facility was opened on 15th street and the department entered a new age of technology.

onthly training to protect the community paid off in more ways than one for Plano's firefighters, who always provided stiff competition in local and regional Fire Pump races. Fire Departments from across the state faced Plano's team at the 1940 Texas State Fair where they brought home a First Place trophy for the title of speediest in the state unwinding and running the hose from truck to hydrant, hooking it up and spraying water through it. A never-before published photograph at bottom of page shows Chief Jim Standerfer collecting the award. Of special note is the extremely rare image of Cotton Landers (standing first left) who remains Plano's only firefighter killed in the line of duty while fighting a fire in 1950.

1940-1949

FIRE RESCUE

Plano Fire Department, 1949 September 15

FIRE
1950-1959
RESCUE

1950 — Plano Population: 2,126

1950 — Clyde E. (Cotton) Landers, 24, dies fighting house fire April 2 becoming only Plano firefighter to date to die in line of duty

1950 — An emergency box was installed at the station containing keys for the fire truck to avoid delays

1951 — The North Texas Municipal Water District is organized with Plano a founding member. Water pumped from Lake Lavon ensures future generations adequate water and fire safety supply

1952 — Department accepted the job of installing City Christmas lights at rate of $100

1952 — Landers Hall, honoring Cotton Landers, dedicated during public ceremony

1953 — 1953 Dodge chassis purchased, mounted with hose bed and pump from wrecked 1942 Dodge Truck with 340-gallon booster tank added. Used for City/County response until 1967

1953 — 1953 GMC 750-gpm truck purchased through the Civil Defense. There are no records to indicate Civil Service ever requested the *Old General's* services

1957 — The Plano Police Department is organized January 1, replacing the City Marshal

1958 — Central Expressway (US75) is completed through Plano to McKinney, considered the single largest factor in Plano's growth

An entire book could be devoted to the gems contained in the department fire minutes. The minutes report fire calls to out-houses, committees formed to assemble oyster suppers, study whether croquet at the fire house should be banned on Sundays, investigate the cost of new curtains for the bathroom and explore whether Fireman Hudson should be allowed to buy the old radio set for $7.50 in cash plus working at the station for a year on donated janitor duty. The minutes also record countless fines levied for abusive language, leaving dominoes on tables, meeting absences, even putting feet on the table during discussion. These fines continued well into the 1950's. On the more serious side drills are detailed on pumper hookup, ladder raising, loading and unloading hoses, how to fight electrical fires, how to operate an iron lung, tie knots and how to ventilate a fire. Not all appointed secretaries enjoyed good penmanship nor spelling. A verbatim entry from 1951 reads "We enjoyed having Brother Syles our knew elected chaplain to meat with us for the first time. We was sorry are present chaplain Brother Parr was absent fore we wood of liked for him to be present to let Brother Syles know just what kind of a bunch he got his self mixed up with."

Families have always been a major component of fire life. They gathered often for picnics and potlucks, strengthening the bonds of community and support. Fire wives willingly assisted with cooking chores for special occasions with public fundraisers often organized solely by the wives of the firemen who donated proceeds for furniture and uniforms. Community support was also strong with Thanksgiving and Christmas bringing an outpouring of special dinners and treats. Even in the 1950's volunteer firemen continued to reach deep into their own pockets for department materials and supplies.

1951 Thanksgiving

1951 Fireman Chicken Supper

FIRE
1950-1959
RESCUE

A 37-year member of the Plano Fire Department, John Dean's name was as familiar to state-wide members of the Texas State Firemen and Fire Marshal's Association as it was to Plano. Dean held every office in the Plano's department including Fire Chief and was honored to serve as President of the State Fireman's Association. For over 20 years he helped conduct the annual Firemen and Fire Marshal's School at Texas A&M. Upon his death in 1966 he was touted as "one of the state's best-known and liked firemen, known throughout state firemen circles as an active, dedicated fireman, vitally interested in the preservation of life and property."

A group of the original "Fire Boys" gather for cards at the station.

1951 Vehicles at City Hall

Firehouse Twins

1st Place Pumper Race, 1958

FIRE
1950-1959
RESCUE

As the department turned 65, an August 1954 *Plano Star Courier* news story touted that Plano "has always had an efficient fire department and has been up front from the standpoint of efficiency and equipment. And now there sits in your fire station a new 750-gallon triple combination pumper, fully equipped. The Ford Emergency truck was purchased in 1949-50 from proceeds earned from the showing of the Gainesville Circus. Thus, at this time, you have at your service 25 Firemen, one 600-gallon pumper, one 500-gallon pumper, one 750-gallon pumper, one 250-gallon auxiliary pump, one Ford Emergency truck, one resuscitator -inhalator, one iron lung and various rescue equipment."

Plano Fire Department
- Organized August 27, 1889 -

Plano, Texas

Community Fire Truck Fund

Receipts as follows
```
Donations    ------------------------ 257.00
Scrap paper  ------------------------  21.85
Transfered form gen.fund ------        30.70
          Total            $ 309.55
```

```
Dx    Disburesments as follows
Carpenter Bros.Parts   ----------    6.55
Murrells hardware      ------------  8.26
Plano,Home and auto    -----------   7.89
C.E.Fleck & Co.        ------------ 281.85
Plano,fire dept.cover bad check      5.00
```

```
          Total       $309.55
```

```
          Bal. 7-11-53      00000
```

FIRE
1950-1959
RESCUE

Former Fire Chiefs Jim Standerfer (1939-1950) and Jim Griffin (1931) chew the fat with then current Fire Chief John Dean as they check out a new foam liquid extinguishing system.

esolutions of Respect pepper the pages of the department's minute books, a tradition of honor dating from the mid-1900's. Current and former volunteers who died outside the line of duty were honored by their Brothers with their families watched over and included in department social functions. This 1954 Resolution reads, "Whereas, it has pleased God to call from this life one our most loyal and worthy Firemen, John F. Jinks, Therefore, be it resolved that we, the Plano Volunteer Fire Department, humbly submit to the will of our Heavenly Father and comfort ourselves with the thought that our loss is His gain. Be it further resolved, That we admonish our members to remember well his loyalty and devotion to this organization and seek to follow his many fine examples that are worthy of emulation. Be it further resolved, That we extend to his Wife, Daughter and other relatives our deepest sympathy and pray that God's richest blessings shall be upon them at all times. And be it further resolved, That a copy of these resolutions be spread on the minutes of this department, a copy be published in the Plano Star Courier and a copy sent to his family. "Signed by Roy Yarbrough, Chaplain; B. H. Garrett, Chief; J. R. Dupree, Lieutenant.

Plano Fireman Killed, 3 Hurt While Fighting Blaze in Home

Special to The Times Herald
Plano, April 3.—One member of the Plano volunteer fire department was killed and three others were injured late Sunday while fighting a blaze in the Negro section of the city.

Clyde E. (Cotton) Landers, 24, was killed when an electricity meter fell from the side of the blazing home and the wires struck him. The three injured firemen, William Lunsford, Clyde Todd and "Toad" Garrett, were reported resting comfortably Monday.

Mr. Landers was taken to St. Paul's Hospital in Dallas where he was given artificial respiration. He failed to revive.

Mr. Landers is an ex-Marine and a former member of the University Park police-force in Dallas.

Funeral services for Mr. Landers will be held at 3 p. m. Tuesday at the First Baptist Church in Plano. Burial will be held at Plano Mutual Cemetery.
...survived by his ...and Clifford Landers of Dallas; Cecil Landers of McKinney and Cletus Landers of Plano.

CLYDE E. (COTTON) LANDERS, 24, PLANO FIREMAN MEETS SUDDEN DEATH WHILE FIGHTING FIRE IN PLANO SUNDAY

Plano and community were saddened late Sunday at the passing of Clyde E. (Cotton) Landers, 24, Plano business man and volunteer fireman who gave his life in the service of others while fighting a fire in the negro section of Plano.

Firemen answered a call Sunday afternoon when the Dulce Guthrie home in the negro section caught fire as wind from an open stove whipped flames from an oil stove through the home, catching curtains and wallpaper on fire and quickly enveloping the house.

Plano volunteer firemen were quickly on the scene. While fighting the blaze, a light meter fell from the burning house and the falling wire struck Mr. Landers. He was rushed to St. Paul Hospital in Dallas, where artificial respiration was administered.

Clyde (Cotton) Landers

He was 24 years, nine months, 24 days old when he died. A former U. S. Marine who saw duty during World War II, he had returned to his home town of Plano where, after a brief stint with the University Park Police Department, he owned and operated Landers Super Service Station.

April 2, 1950 was a balmy spring day and he had started early to arrange new inventory, bay door open to invite in the fresh breeze. Less than a mile away a gust of wind blew through an open screen porch door, whipping soft flames from an oil stove to ignite gently billowing curtains and colorful wallpaper. As fire engulfed the house the sounds of the fire siren sent Clyde (Cotton) Landers scrambling down a ladder, calling out to a waiting patron he'd be back as soon as the fire was out. He ran out his Super Service station door, never to return.

While fighting the blaze with fellow volunteers that included his brother Cletus, a light meter fell from the burning house, sparking falling wires cutting across him. Three others were also injured in the bid to contain the fire: William Lunsford, Clyde Todd and Toad Garrett. The narrow dirt road to the house was clogged with spectators and vehicles delaying the passage of the ambulance desperately trying to navigate down the road. Cotton was rushed to St. Paul's Hospital in Dallas where, despite every effort, he could not be revived.

A popular young man with a promising future from a family with deep Plano roots, Cotton's passing united the community. The lights at the Donley Florist burned into the wee hours leading up to the funeral as tributes and condolences poured in to the Landers family. The local newspaper reported, "The large concourse of sorrowing friends, not only from Plano and community, but from Dallas, McKinney and many other points in Texas and the large and profuse floral offerings attested to the high esteem in which he was held by a host of friends and acquaintances. Plano businesses were closed during his funeral to honor the memory of this gallant fireman, who gave his life unselfishly in the service of others."

On November 2, 1952 Landers Hall was dedicated, a second floor meeting room above the City Hall fire bays, remodeled by the firemen themselves, to honor the memory of their friend, Cotton. To date he is the only Plano fireman to have lost his life in the line of duty, a reminder of the dedication to community exhibited by every responder who answers the call.

...CORATING ...ERS AT CITY HALL LATE 'COTTON' LANDERS

the city Sunday.
work is complete... ...or a dedication... ...ry of Mr. Lan...

Ray Yarbrough informs the Star-Courier that several citizens of Plano and community have subscribed to the fund for this work, which they greatly appreciate. If

PLANO FIREMEN HAVE ABOUT FINISHED IMPROVEMENTS ON MEETING QUARTERS; IN HONOR OF LATE 'COTTON' LANDERS

Showing what cooperation and ...rd work can accomplish, mem... ...Plano Volunteer Fire ...with pride to ...improve... ...ng quarters ...of the Fire

Landers Hall Is Dedicated Sunday Afternoon

Landers Hall was officially dedicated at a public program held in the Firemen meeting quarters, upstairs over the Fire Station, in Sunday afternoon. The Fire...

The Landers Family

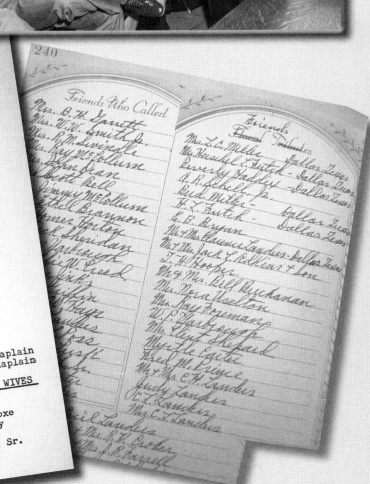

DEDICATION SERVICE OF LANDERS HALL
SUNDAY AFTERNOON NOV. 2, 1952

MASTER OF CEREMONIES		CHIEF GARRET
INVOCATION		FIREMAN YARBROUGH
SONG	"AMERICA"	AUDIENCE
SERVICE RECORD		CHAPLAIN SILER
QUARTETTE		CHAPLAIN POSS
DEDICATION ADDRESS		ASS'T CHIEF DEAN
PRESENTATION		FIREMAN LUSK
BENEDICTION		

PLANO VOLUNTEER FIRE DEPARTMENT

ACTIVE FIREMEN

B. H. Garrett — Chief
John Dean — Ass't Chief
J. R. Dupree — Capt. Co. No. 1
Louis Bourn — Capt. Co. No. 2
Scott Bell — Lt. Co. No. 1
Cletis Landers — Lt. Co. No. 2
R. M. Swindle — Sec.-Treasurer
James Hays
C. B. Painter
J. T. Sheridan
C. C. Oliver
Clyde Todd
John Jinks

Homer Horton
Jimmie McCollom
B. W. Creed
Vernon Lusk
Buddy Brannon
James Todd
Ray McCollom
Mack Spurgin
W. W. Smith, Jr.
W. O. Braden
Dick Spencer
Rev. L. L. Poss, Chaplain
Rev. F. H. Siler, Chaplain

RETIRED FIREMEN

George Good
J. F. Griffin
Earl Wetsel
Joe Starnes
J. H. Standerfer
Ray Yarbrough

DECEASED FIREMEN'S WIVES

Mrs. Gee Hudson
Mrs. W. M. Hedgecoxe
Mrs. L. A. Huguley
Mrs. R. B. Howey
Mrs. W. W. Smith, Sr.

By 1951 the importance of fire safety was being spread to students. Plano's sole high school boasted an active fire prevention committee who regularly met with fire representatives to stage drills and promote fire safety. In 1985 fire education through *Learn not to Burn* became an established part of the Plano Independent School District curriculum.

8-12-1954 - S. COURIER NO. 15

FIRE DEPARTMENT URGES YOUR COOPERATION IN IMPORTANT FIRE PREVENTION CAMPAIGN

Beginning August 14, your Plano Colunteer Fire Department will contact you with information concerning prevention and fire safety. The local Firemen will show you how to help yourself in case you do have a fire and you will be shown fire equipment for home, car, tractor, store, etc.

You will benefit by having extinguishers handy when starts.

Look for a Fireman to call better still call the Fire St and ask for a member to cal demonstrate the extinguisher you. You will help yourself the Fire Department as wel

"They would place this brick somewhere in the school, in various places and then have a fire drill. If you came across the brick, you had to act as if it was where the fire was."

- Paul Mayfield,
Assistant Chief, Retired

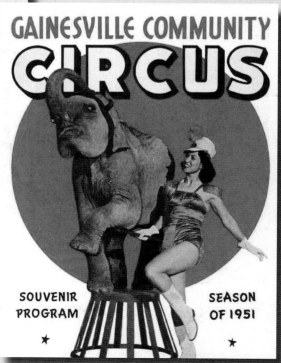

GAINESVILLE COMMUNITY CIRCUS

SOUVENIR PROGRAM ★ ★ SEASON OF 1951

The traveling *Gainesville Community Circus* was a favorite fundraiser for the department, who used the proceeds to aid in the purchase of vehicles and equipment. Unique in that it was presented entirely by amateur residents of Gainesville, Texas, it none-the-less boated three rings including acrobats, trapeze artists, bareback riders, clowns, lions, chimps and an elephant. Always popular with the Plano community, circus proceeds enabled the purchase of a Ford Emergency truck in 1950.

2-6-1954

2-10-54

2 Firemen Injured In Tyler Explosion

Tyler, Feb. 6 (AP).—Dynamite exploded as firemen fought a grass fire here yesterday, injuring two of them.

The dynamite was stored in a concrete septic tank on top of the ground on a lot owned by Tile-Crete Products Co. Heat from the grass fire touched off a dynamite cap, which set off the charge.

The concrete tank disintegrated. Chips from it pierced nearby houses and windows a mile away were broken, police said. The lot is three miles from downtown Tyler.

The two injured firemen were approximately 100 feet away when the dynamite went off. Charles Lawson received head, chest and hand injuries. Doctors amputated three fingers from his left hand. Lt. Luther H. Holt was hospitalized with shock.

Dynamite Victim In Fair Condition

A 9-year-old student at Rocky Crest School in Lancaster whose hands were mangled in the explosion of a dynamite cap was reported in fair condition Thursday at Parkland Hospital.

The youth, Robert Lee Broughtan, was injured about 11:20 a. m. Wednesday when the cap exploded in the packed school room. He told sheriff's deputies he did not know what the cap was.

Treated for minor cuts on the hands and face was Gretel Kirk, teacher, who sheriff's deputies said was injured when she jumped out of a window.

Do you Know if & Where Dynamite & CAPS MIGHT BE STORED IN City?

Grass Fires can be dangerous!

Do you Recognize Dynamite CAPS on SIGHT?

1954 Training Notes

By the 1950's formal training in various fire suppression activities was heavily underway as volunteers faced new challenges with aging infrastructure, abandoned gins and an influx of growth as Plano recovered from the lean war years of the 1940's. Professional trainers were brought in to demonstrate the latest equipment, techniques and new advances in first aid. Departments throughout the region would regularly exchange training materials and host training sessions. The first line of defense continued to be a hose and water, with self-contained breathing apparatus a handkerchief pulled over the nose.

FIRE
1950-1959
RESCUE

Plano Firemen Thank You For Your Donations

'59

Plano Volunteer Firemen appreciate the contributions received from grateful citizens for unselfish service contributed by the firemen at scenes of fires. Among the donations received are those from Henry Jones of Murphy, Mrs. Harriett Hagy of near Plano, and J. F. Harrington and Miss Lula Mae Bailey, of Plano.

These monetary contributions greatly aid the firemen in purchasing needed equipment and provide practically the only source of revenue in securing needed items. If such gifts are not forthcoming they usually have to donate their own personal funds for such purposes.

PLANO FIRE DEPT.

STATE BOARD OF INSURANCE
AUSTIN, TEXAS

DRILL REPORT
of

PLANO   FIRE DEPARTMENT

PLANO,   TEXAS

Quarterly Report for Oct. Nov. & December   19 62

Date	Number of Members Present	Hours of Drill	Description of Drill Work (Give full detail in brief statement)
Oct 2	18	2	Drilled all members present on truck to plug hookups in new areas of City for familiarization of plug locations and problems to be faced in these sections.
Oct 18	14	2	One-half of the members present drilled on plug to truck hookup and the other half drilled on the names of the new streets in the new additions in town.
Nov. 6	20	2	One-half of members present drilled on truck to plug hookups and location and half members present drilled on use of small tools and equipment and their location on the truck.

FIRE RESCUE 1960-1969

By the 1960's Plano was well known for its intensive training and drills. Chief John Dean was selected to conduct classes at the 36th annual Texas Fireman's Training School in 1963 at Texas A&M. Also pictured is Plano City Councilman Lex Newbill who attended the training school as a guest.

1960s Fire Department

Y ou can't keep a good fireman down! Charlie Mays was a frequent presence at the fire house, sharing good advice and memories of how things "used to be." Pictured in 1965, he was an active member of the department from 1900 to 1913.

1960	Plano's population hits 3,695 as it becomes the fastest growing City in Collin County
1960	Lone Star Boat Co. donates boat to Department for lake rescue. A circus is held to raise funds for a motor purchase
1962	Department accepts receipt of new 750-gpm mid-ship pump and high pressure pump Peter Pirsch pumper, equipped with radio
1963	Fire records record 188 fire plugs, four paid firemen and 22 volunteer firemen
1965	28 Plectron home radio receivers improve response time of firemen, enabling them to report directly to fire location
1966	New Central Fire Station and City Hall dedicated August 27. It remains in service today as the City's Technology Services facility, 1117 15th Street
1967	Lee Mayfield becomes Plano's Fire Chief overseeing 8 paid and 19 volunteer firefighters and a Fire Marshal
1967	Department receives a new Fire Appliance Co. of Texas fire truck, replacing the old Dodge fire truck
1969	City Council approves full-time ambulance service by Plano Fire Department after local funeral home discontinues service

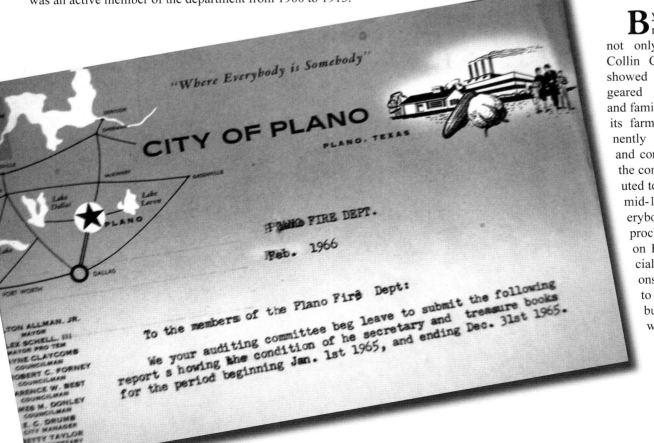

B y the 1960's Plano's municipal letterhead not only touted its prime Collin County location but showed a progressive city geared towards commerce and family. Still holding onto its farming roots, it prominently pictured the cotton and corn that had sustained the community and contributed to its growth since the mid-1800's. "Where Everybody is Somebody" it proclaimed. The typing on February 1966 financial report clearly demonstrates firefighters had to be skilled with a hose but not necessarily with a keyboard!

Members of the Plano Volunteer Fire Department were often honored by members of the community for their service throughout the year. In 1965 Mr. and Mrs. Jim Donley held a turkey dinner and Christmas Party for members of the department, their families and guests. Gifts of cigars, soft drinks and donation checks were often sent to the department in thanks for services rendered by these unpaid heroes.

"Pit fires and the house fire at the Richardson Training Field were the big training items at the time. Diesel was pumped into the pit which was then set on fire making for some very large fires. One of the paint companies in Dallas gave us several barrels of unknown flammable liquids which we poured into the pit and used instead of diesel. These liquids burned with every color under the sun. No one knows what this was or what effect breathing that smoke might have on us."

~ *Carl Dane, Captain, Retired*

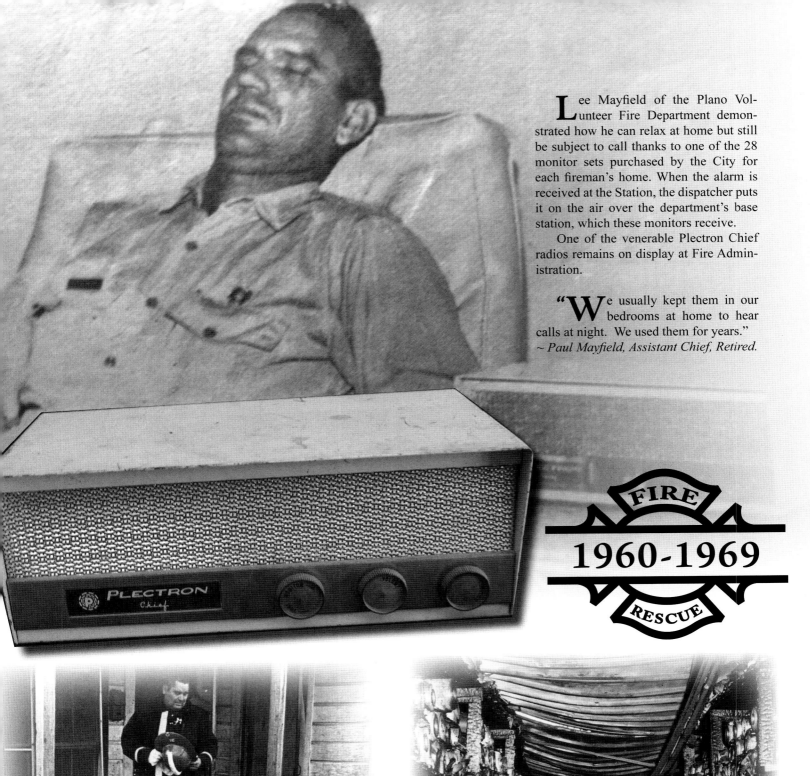

Lee Mayfield of the Plano Volunteer Fire Department demonstrated how he can relax at home but still be subject to call thanks to one of the 28 monitor sets purchased by the City for each fireman's home. When the alarm is received at the Station, the dispatcher puts it on the air over the department's base station, which these monitors receive.

One of the venerable Plectron Chief radios remains on display at Fire Administration.

"We usually kept them in our bedrooms at home to hear calls at night. We used them for years."
~ *Paul Mayfield, Assistant Chief, Retired.*

PLECTRON Chief

FIRE
1960-1969
RESCUE

Early 1966 saw Anhydrous Ammonia fumes spread rapidly across Highway 5 and Central Expressway following the rupture of a one-inch pipe at the Thor Fertilizer Plant. With reports that gas was spewing up to 40 feet in the air, armed with oxygen masks Plano firefighters helped in efforts to shut off the main control valve, evacuate workers and nearby residents and support Police efforts. One Plant employee died from fume inhalation with one Plano firefighter overcome by gas and fumes and treated at a local hospital.

June 3, 1969 Regular Business

Fire Dept. me... ... regular business

Constitution an...

of the...

Plano Fire D...

Plano, T...

CONSTIT...

Article 1...

Section 1. The name of this organi...
THE PLANO FIRE DEPARTMENT, composed ...
gine & Hose ... ... and its motto shall be: "When Duty Calls 'Tis Ours to Obey."

Article 2. Members—Election

Section 1. Any male ... person of good moral character who has attained the age of 21 years and resides ... is eligible to membership in this department.

Section 2. The initiation fee into the departmen... shall be Two ($2.00) Dollars. Persons wishing to be... come members of the department must apply by letter... stating age, accompanied by the initiation fee, plus one... half cost of uniform, addressed to the officers and mem...

3. ... and...

interview...

1966 Well Discovery

Members of the Plano Volunteer Fire Department had a brush with history as one of the original 1900's downtown fire wells was discovered when making road improvements in front of the new central fire station in 1966. Still holding water, it was pumped dry and filled to enable construction to proceed.

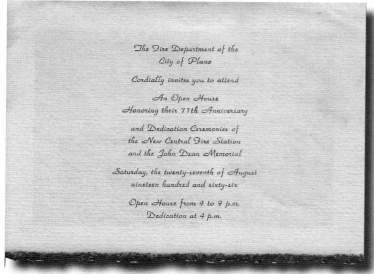

Hundreds of residents turned out for the dedication of the new Central Fire Station and John Dean Memorial August 27, 1966. Senator Ralph Hall gave a keynote address with Fire Chief Lee Mayfield joining the Mayor and representatives of the Fireman's Association in commemorating former Fire Chief John Dean through the naming of a recreation room in his honor. The ceremony coincided with the opening of the adjacent new Plano City Hall. The station boasted lecture rooms, air conditioned living quarters for 22 persons, a shop, five bays, a fully equipped kitchen, modern bath facilities and a recreation room. Central Fire remained at this location until 1994 when the current stand-alone Station 1 and Fire Administration facility opened at 1901 K Avenue. The footprint of the facility still remains, now housing the City's Technology Services Department.

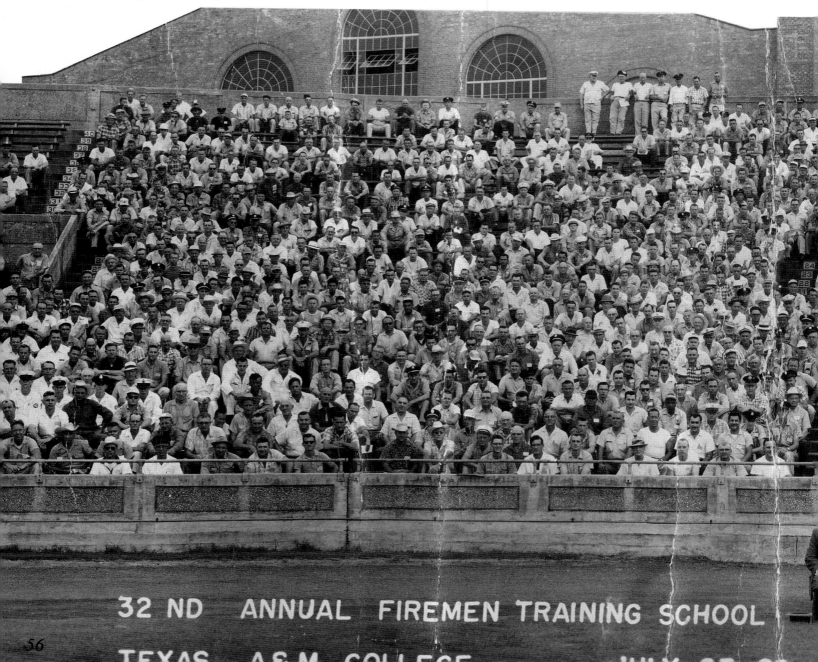

32 ND ANNUAL FIREMEN TRAINING SCHOOL

TEXAS A&M COLLEGE

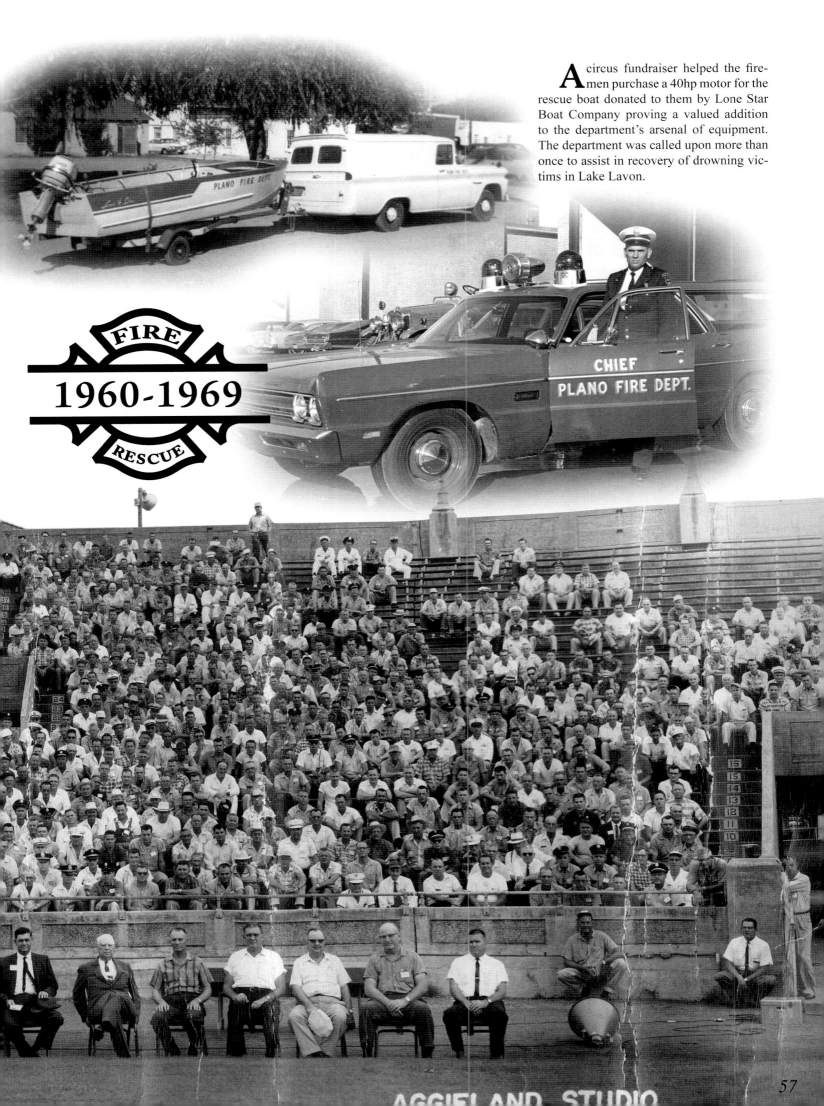

A circus fundraiser helped the firemen purchase a 40hp motor for the rescue boat donated to them by Lone Star Boat Company proving a valued addition to the department's arsenal of equipment. The department was called upon more than once to assist in recovery of drowning victims in Lake Lavon.

FIRE

1960-1969

RESCUE

CHIEF
PLANO FIRE DEPT.

AGGIELAND STUDIO

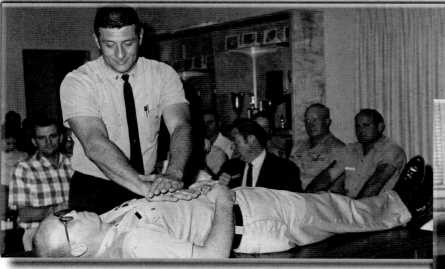

1965 saw Plano firemen receive lessons in mouth-to-mouth resuscitation and heart massage, including practicing first-aid techniques on a state-of-the-art training tool, a lady dummy named "Resusca Ann."

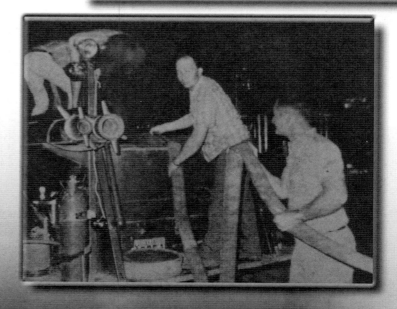

The first Tuesday and third Thursday of each month were practice nights for the department's volunteers and paid firemen who drilled four hours per month. Loading and reloading the fire trucks was a popular practice geared towards increasing response time and fostering teamwork.

"Back when I was hired on, if you could physically walk up to the front door and had enough sense to open it, you were qualified to be hired."
~ Paul Mayfield, Assistant Chief, Retired

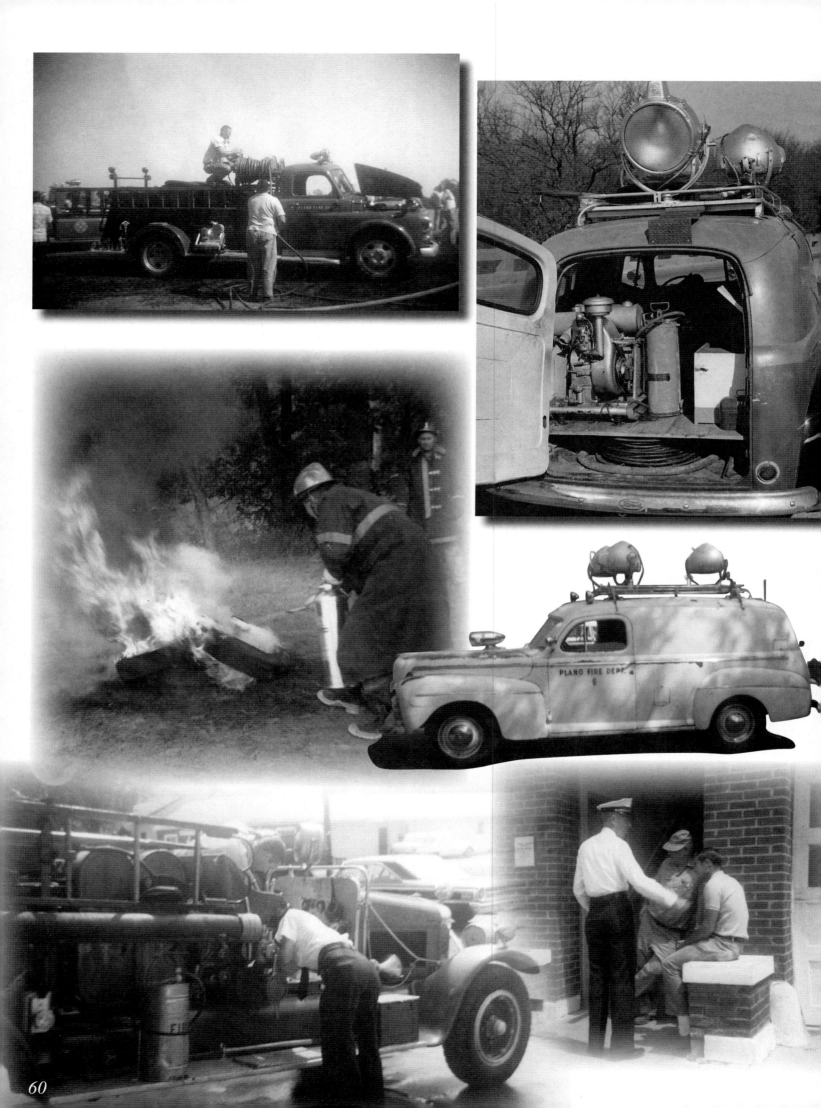

FIRE 1960-1969 RESCUE

EST ADDITION to the Volunteer Fire Department is the new pumper truck.
as a 750 gallon pump and also a high pressure pump. It carries 550 gallons
ater and 1500 inches of 2½ inch hose, 450' of 1½ inch hose, 300' of 1
high pressure hose and is radio equipped. Shown at the helm is Scott
one of the city's four paid firemen. Others are B. H. Garrett, Paul May-
d and Mac Spurgin. (Photo by L. W. Cason).

PLANO FIRE DEPT.

PLANO FIRE DEPT.

FIRE MARSHALL Scott Bell, left, and Fireman Wayne Yandell demonstrate the three ways to extinguish a kitchen grease fire. According to Fire Marshall Bell, a grease fire can be extinguished by throwing baking soda on the flames, hand fire extinguisher, or by covering the pan or skillet with a lid.

June 2, 1969 VFD

Fire Dept. met in regular

night June 3, 1969

preceding

Chaplain Grigg

were present

meetings read

Constitution and By-Laws
of the

Plano Fire Department

Plano, Texas

CONSTITUTION

Article 1—Name

Section 1. The name of this organization shall be THE PLANO FIRE DEPARTMENT, composed of Engine & Hose and its motto shall be: "When Duty Calls 'Tis Ours to Obey."

Article 2. Members—Election

Section 1. Any male person of good moral character who has attained the age of 21 years and resides is eligible to membership in this department.

Section 2. The initiation fee into the department shall be Two ($2.00) Dollars. Persons wishing to become members of the department must apply by letter, stating age, accompanied by the initiation fee, plus one-half cost of uniform, addressed to the officers and members of The Plano Fire Department of Plano, Texas, bearing their proper signatures and recommended by three members as a man of good moral character. The applicant shall then be balloted for and if no more than three black balls appear shall be declared duly elected a member of this department.

Section 3. The membership of this Department shall be not more than twenty-five active members.

Article 3: Officers—Election

Section 1. The officers of this department shall consist of a Chief and an Assistant Chief, Secretary-Treasurer, and the Captain and Lieutenant of each

1. ... Companies No. 1, No. 2, and No. 3,

2. ... within the city limits of PLANO ...

3. ... and action of the interview committee.

4. serve a 6 months probationary period. He shall then be balloted for and if no more than three black balls appear shall ...

5. less

Handwritten 1969 Changes to Bylaws

FIRE
1960-1969
RESCUE

MORE THAN 600 STUDENTS CLEAR SCHOOL BUILDING IN 78 SECONDS IN FIRE DRILL; FIREMEN CONGRATULATE PUPILS

A total of 618 Senior and grammar school students in the Plano school cleared the big school building in one minute and 18 seconds in a fire drill Thursday afternoon.

Taking one of the fire trucks to the school, Chief John Dean and other members of the local department sponsored the drill a ——

succession brings the children to attention as the signal for a fire or fire drill. The students did not know whether it was practice drill or a real fire. They spend 15 minutes per week in fire drills.

The High School has a fire department of its own, with Don Ren—— Chief; Kenneth Braden,

PLANO FIRE MARSHALL SCOTT BELL is putting up display posters stressing National Fire Prevention Week, to be observed in Plano October 3-9.

Fire Department Picnic

Plano, Texas
1963

"The town was small enough that everyone knew everyone and that helped with the sending of calls. One night a house was on fire and the girl said to send the fire department. When the operator asked where, the girl just said 'Just tell Paul. He knows where I live.'"

~ Paul Mayfield,
Assistant Chief, Retired

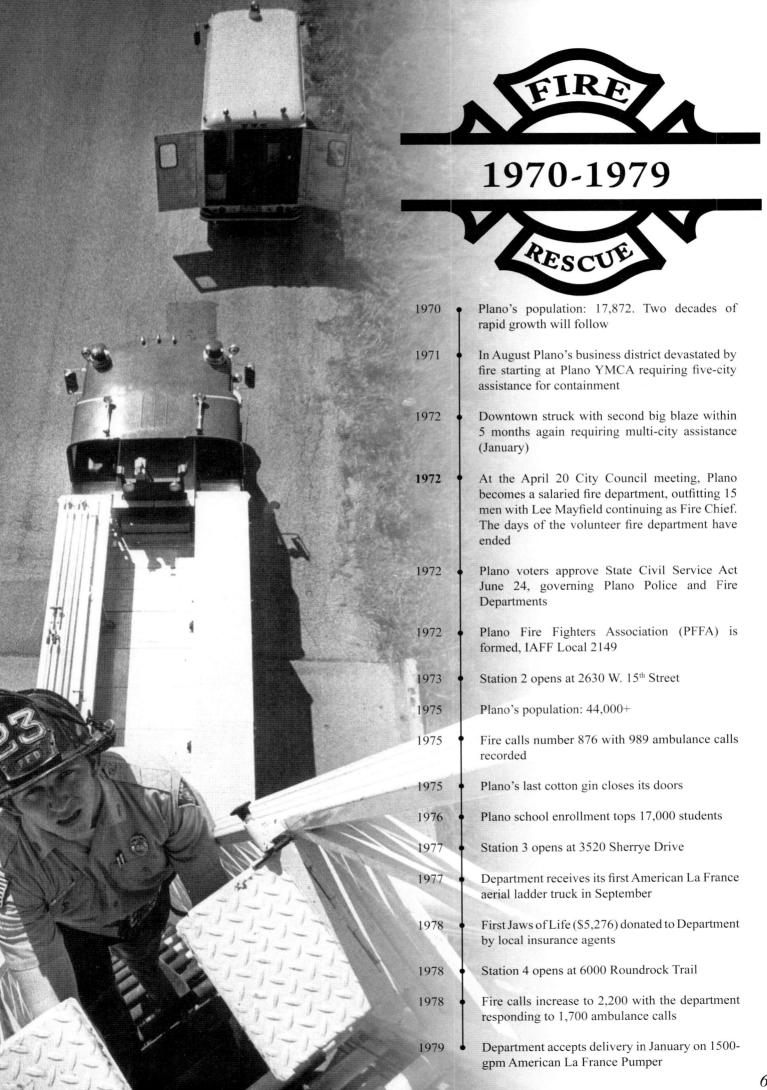

FIRE
1970-1979
RESCUE

1970	Plano's population: 17,872. Two decades of rapid growth will follow
1971	In August Plano's business district devastated by fire starting at Plano YMCA requiring five-city assistance for containment
1972	Downtown struck with second big blaze within 5 months again requiring multi-city assistance (January)
1972	At the April 20 City Council meeting, Plano becomes a salaried fire department, outfitting 15 men with Lee Mayfield continuing as Fire Chief. The days of the volunteer fire department have ended
1972	Plano voters approve State Civil Service Act June 24, governing Plano Police and Fire Departments
1972	Plano Fire Fighters Association (PFFA) is formed, IAFF Local 2149
1973	Station 2 opens at 2630 W. 15th Street
1975	Plano's population: 44,000+
1975	Fire calls number 876 with 989 ambulance calls recorded
1975	Plano's last cotton gin closes its doors
1976	Plano school enrollment tops 17,000 students
1977	Station 3 opens at 3520 Sherrye Drive
1977	Department receives its first American La France aerial ladder truck in September
1978	First Jaws of Life ($5,276) donated to Department by local insurance agents
1978	Station 4 opens at 6000 Roundrock Trail
1978	Fire calls increase to 2,200 with the department responding to 1,700 ambulance calls
1979	Department accepts delivery in January on 1500-gpm American La France Pumper

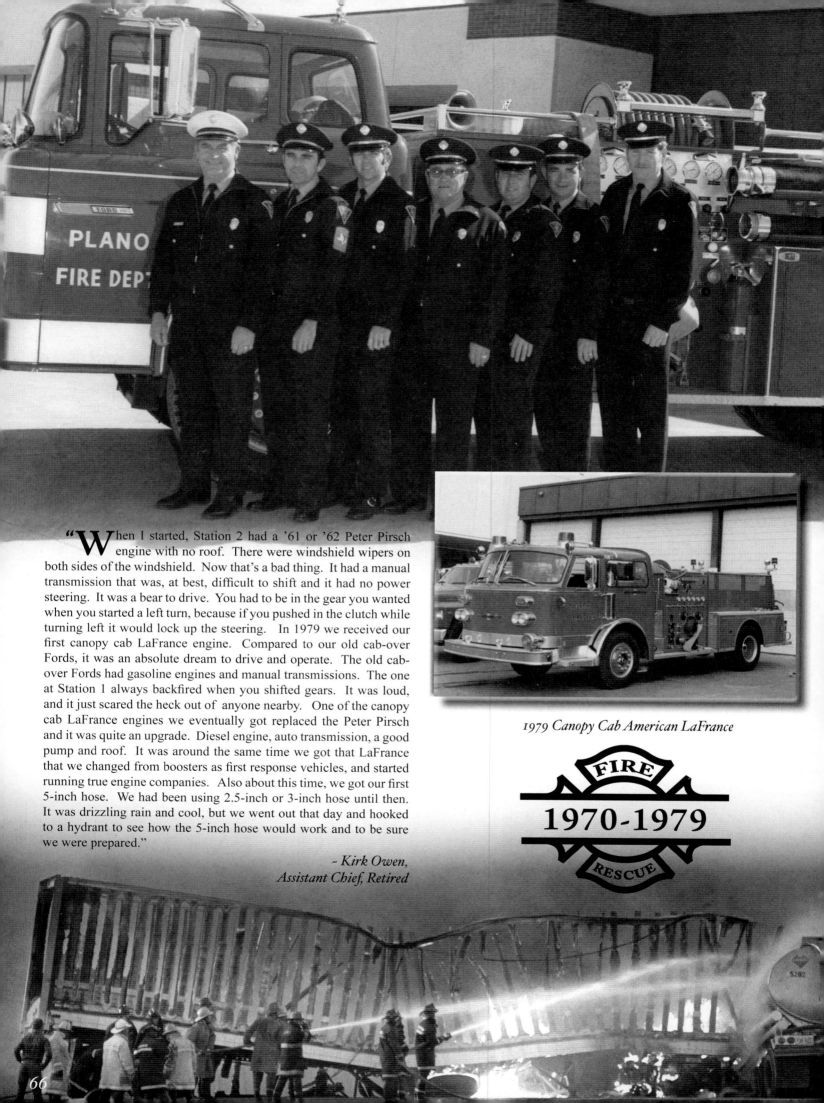

"When I started, Station 2 had a '61 or '62 Peter Pirsch engine with no roof. There were windshield wipers on both sides of the windshield. Now that's a bad thing. It had a manual transmission that was, at best, difficult to shift and it had no power steering. It was a bear to drive. You had to be in the gear you wanted when you started a left turn, because if you pushed in the clutch while turning left it would lock up the steering. In 1979 we received our first canopy cab LaFrance engine. Compared to our old cab-over Fords, it was an absolute dream to drive and operate. The old cab-over Fords had gasoline engines and manual transmissions. The one at Station 1 always backfired when you shifted gears. It was loud, and it just scared the heck out of anyone nearby. One of the canopy cab LaFrance engines we eventually got replaced the Peter Pirsch and it was quite an upgrade. Diesel engine, auto transmission, a good pump and roof. It was around the same time we got that LaFrance that we changed from boosters as first response vehicles, and started running true engine companies. Also about this time, we got our first 5-inch hose. We had been using 2.5-inch or 3-inch hose until then. It was drizzling rain and cool, but we went out that day and hooked to a hydrant to see how the 5-inch hose would work and to be sure we were prepared."

- Kirk Owen,
Assistant Chief, Retired

1979 Canopy Cab American LaFrance

FIRE

1970-1979

RESCUE

1973 Station 2

PLANO FIRE DEPARTMENT

- *Organized August 27, 1889* -

PLANO, TEXAS
JANUARY 1, 1970

To the members of the Pla...

We your audi... submit the following r...
conditi... ...ooks for the period b...
1969 and...

Receipts...

Cash on ha... ...Texas; Jan. 1st 19...
Dues--------
Coca Cola-------
Fines-----------
Donations-------
Decals----------
City Fire Fin...
Applications---
County Fires----
      misc   in...   Total Rec...

UNIFORM FIRE CODE

1979 EDITION

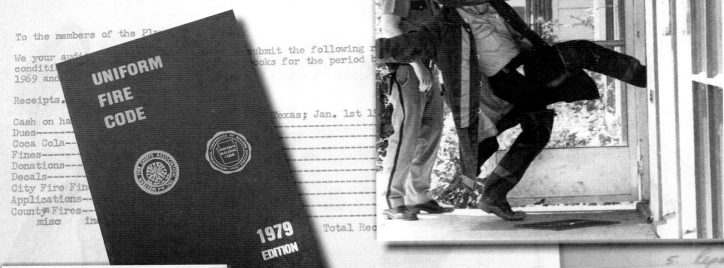

Dec. 31s...
...af Fund
...tional B...
...aving an...

```
            Firemen Attending Fires
                   May 1971

Cliff Spears          1        $5.00
S.R. Davidson         1         5.00
Eldon Dyer            1         5.00
Dale Martin           1         5.00
Doyle Spurgin         1         5.00
Ray Rogers            1         5.00
Larry Dunlap          1         5.00
John West             1         5.00
Charles Robinson      1         5.00
George Gunter         1         5.00
Len Rush              1         5.00
Dwayne Brazil         1         5.00
Mack Spurgin          1         5.00
Kenneth Sartain       1         5.00
Sam Sartain           1         5.00
James Shanks          1         5.00
Scott Bell            1         5.00
Gene Pell             1         5.00
                     ---       ------
                     18       $90.00

Date 5-11-71          Location:  3417 Ave. N
```

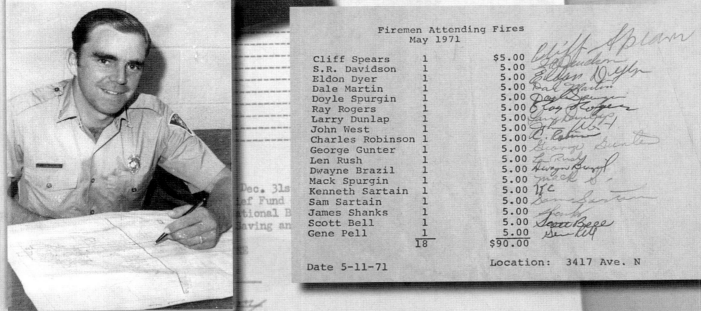

1977 Station 3

"To make the most of the long hours at the station, Robert Westbrook and myself bought a set of encyclopedias. Each shift we would select a volume and page at random and read about whatever was there. We would research that subject to the best of our ability. (Before the internet and computers, that is.) One day the subject was capacitors and how they are constructed. We could not believe that a small capacitor held a hundred yards of aluminum-backed Mylar inside. We went to the auto parts store, purchased one, cut it open, and started unrolling it. Someone came up with a bat kite and we attached the Mylar as a tail and continued to unroll the aluminum as we let the kite fly higher.

There really is that much Mylar in a capacitor. The tail of the kite was glittering in the sun as it flew higher and higher. When we came to the end of the string, we sent the ambulance down to Skaggs for more, which we added and continued to let it out. We eventually had our kite so high that only the flashing tail could be seen, somewhere out above the hospital. We began to worry about the radar from D/FW picking us up so be brought it down. This took several hours to let out and reel back in. I don't know what would have happened if a call had come in while we had almost two miles of string flying in the air."

- Carl Dane
Captain, Retired

FIRE
1970-1979
RESCUE

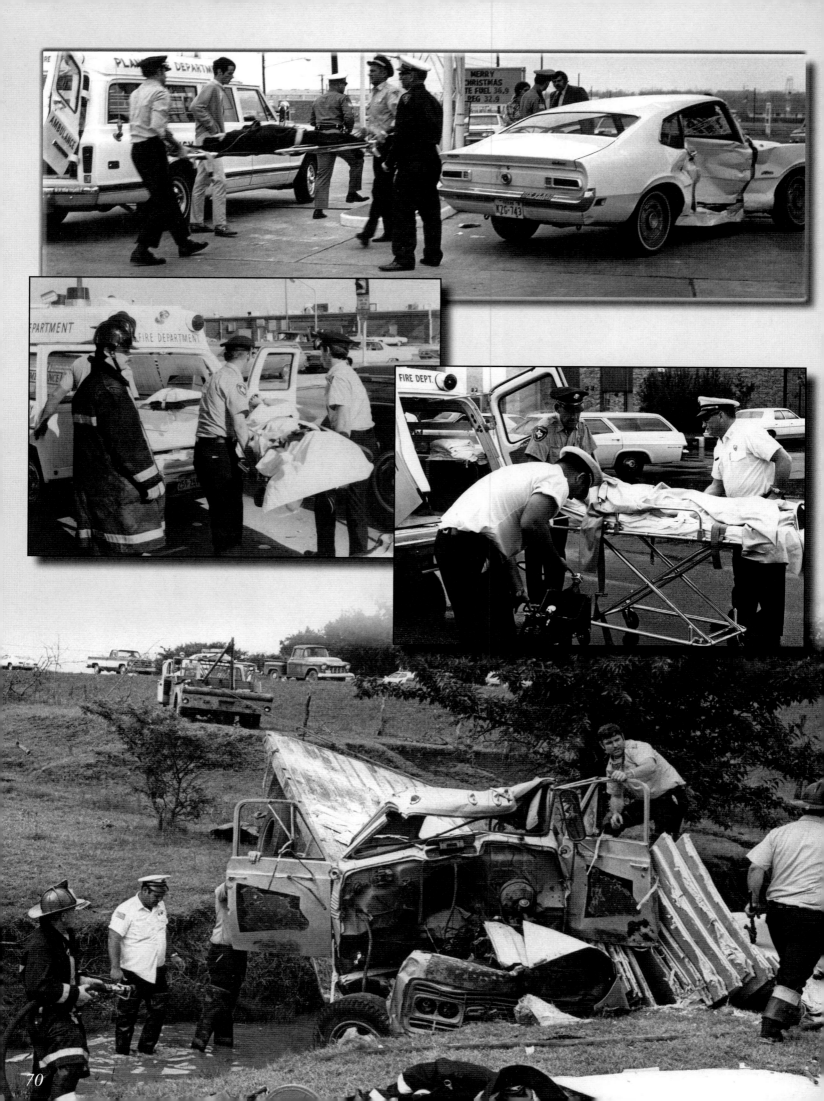

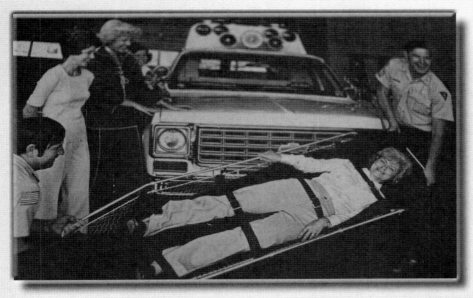

F irefighters gained a valued new weap-on in firefighting, and more important-ly in personal safety, when the department's first self-contained breathing apparatus units arrived on the scene. An original unit is on display in Fire Administration.

MEMBERS OF THE PLANO FIRE DE-PARTMENT received their sevice pins at the Department's Christmas party December 9 at the Fire Station which was attended by Plano firemen and their families. Fire Marshall Scott Bell, first row, left, received a twenty year pin; Lynn Rush, one year; Jimmy Davidson, one year; Eldon Dyer, five years; Mack Spurgin, second row, left, twenty; Fire Chief Lee Mayfield, fifteen years; Dwayne Brazel, one year; Charles Robinson, five years; E.E. Rittenberry, five years; and Richard Stout, one year.

FIRE
1970-1979
RESCUE

1978 Station 4

Smoke Alarms Prevent Would-Be Tragedies

At least one Plano family is a walking advertisement for the benefits of a smoke alarm.

The Perris M. Stanley family was awakened from a deep sleep last January by their alarm which had only been in place a few weeks.

Although Stanley was unable to smell any smoke himself, he got his family out of the house, called the fire department and made a careful search of the home.

He discovered the garage fire on his second, closer look around the residence. Even though barely detectable at that point, it had already spread to the attic.

The home sustained major damage, but the family was safe. Fire Marshal Bill Threet credits the smoke alarm for averting a possible tragedy.

The melted detector—which still works—is now a prize exhibit for his Fire Prevention Week activities. Threet firmly believes in this year's slogan that "Where There's Smoke....There Should Be A Smoke Alarm."

"Most fatality and injury fires happen at night between 9 p.m. and 6 a.m.," explained Threet. "Usually these fires start in upholstered furniture or a mattress and smolder for hours before bursting into flame.

"Smoke detectors sense the smoke and sound an alarm giving you time to escape," he added. "A great majority of fire victims are not burned, they are overcome by the poisonous gases without even waking. Most deaths occur in the early stages of the fire.

The r...

detector is that it gives an early warning of an impending fire, noted Inspector Bill Gentry. Those few minutes of time are precious when it comes to getting out of the house.

"Life safety is the main reason to have smoke alarms," he continued, "But having one can also cut down on property damage. Those extra few minutes may be the time we need to get the blaze out before it causes extensive damage."

From time to time, the department gets a call on a smoke alarm going off without an obvious cause, Threet noted. An investigation often reveals a condition, such as an overheated motor, which might have led to a fire if not corrected.

There is a large selection of smoke alarms on the market today, and Threet recommends that residents purchase alarms from a reputable retail dealer, avoiding door to door sales.

The smoke alarm should have UL (Underwriter Laboratory) or F.M. (Factory Mutual) approval, he stressed. Most detectors range from $25 to $45, although sales are conducted periodically.

There are two types of alarms and several power source options, according to Gentry. Models are available which run on battery power, that are wired into household current, that plug into a conventional electrical outlet or that use a combination

the alarm.

Ionization devices produce electrically charged air molecules which cause a small electric current to flow in the chamber. Smoke particles entering the detector attach themselves to the ions, reducing the electrical flow which sets off the alarm.

"Both types of smoke detectors are reliable," Threet affirmed. "There is no evidence that one is more effective than the other. Both types are approved by testing laboratories and each does a good job.

"A detector should be installed between the living and sleeping areas of a home," he added. "If there is more than one sleeping area, then another detector is needed."

Although the alarms put out 85 decibels of sound, experts recommend that the detectors should be mounted close enough to the bedrooms that the alarm can be heard with the doors shut. Homes with two levels should have detectors mounted at the head of the stairs.

Threet stressed that corners should be avoided since "dead air spaces" are created in the area within six inches of the corner.

Having a family escape plan is as important as the detector, Gentry pointed out. The lack of oxygen in a fire makes people drowsy and the danger of panic is always present.

"People should plan ahead to have ... out of every room," he ... re may ... ought ... eting ... eople

Page 3

"**A**nother common drill was the Church Raise with the 35 foot extension ladder. We would set this up in the parking lot behind Station 2 and each man would have to climb up one side, over the top, and down the other side. I'm not sure what this was teaching us to do as I could not think of any good reason that this could be applied to on the fire ground. Captain Brazil said it was to give you confidence in the other men. That could be debatable but we did it almost every month as a drill."

- Carl Dane
Captain, Retired

The Plano Post

HELPING PLANO AND COLLIN COUNTY TO GROW

Thursday, August 26, 1971

Blaze Destroys Downtown Buildings

By Guy Marble
Editor

A massive multi-alarm fire gutted a square block of downtown Plano Wednesday night wiping out four business operations and the YMCA. Initial estimates place the loss at $100,000, according to Fire Marshall Scott Bell.

Curious Mob Crowds Scene

By Laura Hobart
Post Staff

Curious spectators crowding the scene of Wednesday night's blaze hampered police

Destroyed in the blaze were the YMCA, Hometown Furniture, McKee's Air Conditioning, Howard's Welding and the House of Carpets rug warehouse.

Every unit from the local department, plus equipment from Richardson, McKinney, Wylie, Frisco and Allen battled the blaze for two hours before bringing the fire under control.

Seven firemen were injured and six were hospitalized over night at Richardson General. H.H. Atkins of Plano was the only fireman not released this morning. He is reported in good condition at the hospital.

The initial alarm was reported to firemen just before 7 p.m. and the first u-

that gathered to watch. Spectators reported seeing smoke and fire from as far away as McKinney and Garland.

Mayfield estimated it was about 9 p.m. before the holocaust was under control, although firemen stayed at the scene all night to prevent a possible flareup of the remains.

Two men fighting the blaze, Richard Stout of Plano and Chief Bill Storey of Wylie, received severe cuts in the firefighting. Stout's leg required 40 stitches.

Chief Mayfield praised the work of all men fighting the blaze characterizing their work as "outstanding." Mayfield also praised many private citizens who assisted firemen at the scene. The

FIRE
1970-1979
RESCUE

This smoke alarm may have saved the lives of the Perris M. Stanley family last year. The detector, which melted in the 1976 blaze, is a prize exhibit of Fire Prevention Week. Firefighters across the nation are urging homeowners to buy smoke alarms which can be the needed margin of safety in night fires. Fire Marshal Bill Threet, right, and Inspector Bill Gentry spend much of their time explaining how a smoke alarm can save a life. To arrange a program, call 424-7875. (Staff photo by Mike Newman).

"Just for something to do, one day we went into another shift's food locker and removed all of their can goods. We took an Exacto knife and removed all the labels, shuffled them around and re-glued them on the cans."

- Carl Dane
Captain, Retired

"And I do," he said.
"We had planned to go through the office area this morning," said Botts, pointing to a heap of smoldering wood, "but they have scrapped all of the trash from the street on top of it."

ing at least ... false alarm ... dents, and a false alarm at the Timber Forest Apts. Chief Toler said, however, that the accidents were due to the weather conditions rather than the fire.

Shop Owner 'Counts Blessings'

By Joann Voiers
Post Staff

"We certainly are counting our blessings this morning," said Joyce Kennedy, owner of the Kennedy Wig Salon which is located in the Adams Professional Bldg.

The fire which devastated many nearby stores did relatively little damage to Mrs. Kennedy's place of business.

"I had just gone home when Mrs. Schumacher (Iva Schumacher of Tam-Trac Realty, ... in the Adams ... everyone she ... to tell ... was

the smoke smell is gone," Joyce continued, "but we will be alright. Yes, we were very lucky."

"I just don't know what we would have done without those kids," claimed Iva Schumacher. "Why, those big boys came right in and carried all our supplies, desks, chairs, everything right out to safety."

Putting things in order today, Mr. and Mrs. Schumacher reflected on the courage and stamina of local police and firemen, adding that the situation could have been much worse.

Hanging on the door of the office of Dr. Ernest Lontos, an orthodontist, also located in the Adams Bldg. was the ... simple sign: Closed Due to

77

1970-1979

"Falling into the 'it seemed like a good idea at the time' category, we held three benefit firefighters rodeos with proceeds assisting firefighters or their families who were in need. It took a lot of work to put these on and a majority of the department was involved, with the Firefighters Association sponsoring events and help from local businesses. The rodeos were two-night events held at the John Coomer Memorial Arena in Wylie and involved other area fire departments. At least one year I remember we held a dance with a live band after the rodeo each night at the Wylie Gin. They were a tremendous amount of fun and fellowship, although the unsanctioned cow riding event for selected spouses held after the dance one year was a bad idea!"

*-Kirk Owen,
Assistant Chief, Retired*

PLANO FIREFIGHTERS BENEFIT

RODEO

FRIDAY & SATURDAY
MAY 4 & 5

★ **BAREBACK**

★ **BULL RIDING**

★ **OPEN BARREL RACE**

★ **WILD HORSE RACE**

BOOKS OPEN:
BARREL RACING ONLY
Wed., May 2
12 Noon,
Close 6 P.M.
Phone 596-3605

★ **DANCES** ★
DANCE EACH NIGHT AT THE
WYLIE GIN. FEATURING
PEGGY REEVES AND HER BAND

ALL PROCEEDS GO TO PLANO FIREFIGHTERS RELIEF FUND

JOHN COOMER MEMORIAL ARENA

HWY. 544 at FM 1378   **WYLIE, TEXAS**   Stock Produced by West Rodeo Co

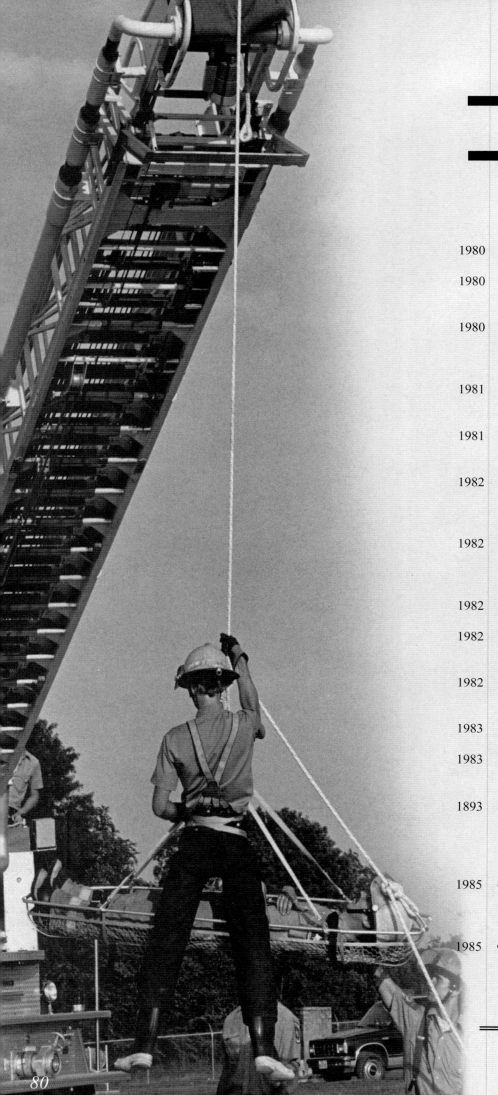

1980	●	Plano population: 72,331
1980	●	Bus service comes to Plano from Dallas Area Rapid Transit
1980	●	New City Hall opens at 1520 K Avenue, known as Plano Municipal Center. Fire remained at the 15th street old city hall adjacent the new building
1981	●	Gulf Tanker unloading fuel at Parker/U. S. 75 ignites in conflagration
1981	●	Passage of new fire code includes raising arson reward to $1,000
1982	●	Lee Mayfield retires in January after 16 years as Chief and 25 years as a firefighter. Continues service in Fire Marshal's office
1982	●	Department receives two additional American La France pumper engines and a second Water Chief American La France aerial ladder truck
1982	●	EMS Paramedic services begins in Plano in June
1982	●	First Ticknor harness is purchased in May for rescue operations
1982	●	In November William E. Peterson, Waheegan, IL., named Fire Chief
1983	●	Station 5 opens at 5115 W. Park Boulevard
1983	●	First outdoor emergency warning sirens installed at fire stations as tornado warning
1893	●	Paramedic Engine Companies are established in October, the final result of complete cross-training of all civil service employees in fire, rescue, EMS and public education
1985	●	Ken Klein is hired as department's first emergency medical services coordinator in January
1985	●	Opticom traffic signal system installation begins in February enabling manipulation of traffic signals for emergency response vehicles

"**E**ach home in Plano received a free roll of garbage bags twice a year. The fire stations got the privilege to pass these out. A card was mailed to each house and the owner could bring this by the station for a free roll. It was not unusual for Station 2 to give away two or three hundred rolls and sell another hundred during the summertime on weekends.

Sometimes people would return a roll that had not been divided and was one continual roll. We used some of this plastic to make a box kite that was eight feet tall and three feet on a side. It flew like a dream. We even made the front page of the *Plano Star Courier* with it."

- Carl Dane
Captain, Retired

1983 Station 5

Caldwell at Scene with ALF

Plano firemen battle blaze
Saturday at mini-warehouse

Gusty winds played havoc for Plano firemen Saturday as they fought to stop a three-alarm fire that swept through several mini-warehouse units at 1100 Plano Parkway.

As a large group of spectators watched, 11 units with 29 men from four Plano fire stations tried to stop the

flames, reported at 12:17 p.m.

The firemen's work was delayed because they had to break through locks of each warehouse door in order to contain the blaze, which destroyed approximately 30 warehouse units.

Fire Marshal Bill Threet has not yet determined the

cause of the blaze or the dollar loss.

Firemen John Housewright and Ronnie Price were treated for minor injuries at the scene while Larry Farmer was treated for a knee injury and released from Plano General Hospital.

Initially, firefighters could only get to the flames by cutting holes in the doors. (Staff photo by Mike Newman).

—Plano Daily Star-Courier—Wednesday, December 9, 1981

ARSON REWARD

Ordinance 81-8-11 Section XV. The City of Plano offers a reward of One Thousand Dollars ($1,000.00), for the arrest and conviction of any person found guilty of committing the crime of arson within the corporate limits of the City. This reward is a standing offer, and shall be paid out of the General Fund of the City.

Information concerning the following arson cases may be given to investigators by calling the Fire Marshal at 424-6531, extension 5430.

1. 1974 Chevrolet half-ton pick-up, November 18, 1981, 9:30 p.m. - 7:30 a.m.	1408 Quill Drive	November 19, 1981
2. Dwelling	2701 Kingston Drive	October 26, 1981
3. Dwelling	1721 Debbie Drive	July 24, 1981
4. 1980 Firebird Pontiac	North Star Road, near 14th Street	July 15, 1981
5. Dwelling	1521 Lorraine Drive	July 6, 1981
6. Boat	1525 Cross Bend Road	December 20, 1980

Health problems cause Mayfield to step down

By PAM TROBOY
Staff Writer

PLANO—Fire Chief Lee Mayfield has stepped down for health reasons. Beginning 30 days of sick leave today at the instigation of his physician, Mayfield plans to take "some time to get it back together."

"It has been very evident to me and my doctor that the stress is not doing my health any good," he said. "It's in my and my family's best interest that I resign."

"This is not something that has come up overnight," he admitted. "I have known for some time that this was coming.

"I spent 48 hours in the hospital this week, discussing it with my doctor, my wife and myself. It was a very hard decision to make, but it's a decision I finally made."

Although he is no longer physically able to serve as chief of the 115-man unit, Mayfield will return to the Fire Department in some capacity on Feb. 22.

"We will determine his role at that time," said City Manager David Griffin. "We know it will be a valuable one.

"His experience and knowledge should not be wasted," he stressed. "We ought to get the benefit of that."

LEE MAYFIELD

For over four decades the name *Mayfield* filled the fire logs. Brothers Lee and Paul hired on as firefighters and later served as Fire Chief and Assistant Chief. From left to right in photo:

- Lee Mayfield, Plano's Fire Chief from 1966 to 1982.
- Terry Mayfield, son of Lee Mayfield. Terry was the Assistant Fire Marshal for the McKinney Fire Department and the Fire Chief in Seguin.
- Jackie Mayfield, younger brother to Paul and Lee Mayfield. Jackie served as the Training Officer for the Richardson Fire Department and the Fire Chief for the Coppell, Sherman and Cedar Hill Fire Departments.
- Paul Mayfield, known as "Two Chief," was hired as a Plano firefighter in 1960, was promoted to Assistant Chief in 1972 and retired in 1990.
- Paul Mayfield says of his brother, "Lee lived and done by the fire department. It was his life."

Former Plano fire chief dies

By BUCK WARGO
Staff Writer

Lee Mayfield, Plano's first paid fire chief who worked in the department for 26 for years, died Monday at his residence in Dike, Texas. He was 56.

Mayfield started as a volunteer with the Plano Fire Department in 1956 and was eventually hired in 1963. He became chief in August 1966 and held that position until he resigned due to health reasons in 1982.

During his tenure as chief, Mayfield opened four fire stations in Plano and helped the paramedic program get started.

He helped develop a mutual training field with the Richardson Fire Department. That field today is known as the Mayfield-Russell Fire Training Center.

"He obviously set the groundwork that guided the growth of the department," said current Fire Chief William Peterson.

After he resigned as chief, Mayfield worked in the City of Plano fire marshall's office as an arson investigator until he retired in 1985.

Those who knew Mayfield said he was an affable person. He was

known by some of the firefight[...] as a father figure and called "D[...] Lee," said assistant fire ch[...] George Caldwell.

"He was a very personable [...] of individual who would liste[...] what you had to say and be [...] frank about his opinion," Cal[...] said.

Mayfield was twice ch[...] Plano's "Citizen of the Year." Before giving the award [...] night, the speaker told the aud[...] that "Lee's work is a vocation, [...] job." The speaker went on '[...]

Turn to MAYFIELD, pag[...]

Lee Mayfield

Doctors say paramedics saved two lives

Plano's new program already proven successful

By PAM TROBOY
Staff Writer

PLANO—Doctors believe two people are alive today because of Plano's new paramedics program.

"The paramedics have been a tremendous addition to this community health service-wise," praised Dr. Wayne Roop, medical director of emergency services at Plano General Hospital.

"They are providing a great proficiency of pre-hospital care," he said. "We have directly attributed the lives of two patients to the paramedics.

"Both were heart attack victims," Roop explained. "The paramedics were influential in saving these lives and that service was not available prior to this month."

Although the paramedics take their field orders from doctors at Parkland Hospital, most of the patients still request treatment at PGH.

The city decided to join the greater Dallas area system because the existing program has specialists at the teaching hospital available 24 hours a day.

The manpower burden would be too great for PGH now, but Roop predicted that a Plano base station for Collin County communities may be possible in a few years.

About three or four patients a day have benefited from treatment by paramedics during the first month, according to Roop, with operations "remarkably trouble-free."

Acting Fire Chief Paul Mayfield agrees. He said the men have had some trouble with their portable radios, but the problem should be resolved next week.

"I've been real pleased with the program," he said. "For my part, things have gone real good...especially when you consider the cost."

When the city first considered adding paramedics, he explained, the cost was estimated at about $700,000. If the city had begun with a full program, the Fire Department would have lost 21 men to paramedics school.

By trickling the program in, Mayfield pointed out, the department has been able to absorb much of the overtime which would otherwise have been required.

The city began paramedic service on Aug. 2 with seven men (one with prior training) qualified. Curren[tly] they operate out of Central Stati[on] downtown Plano.

Ambulances are used as [first] responders" to medical emerg[ency] in three of the four districts w[ith] paramedics answering centra[lly] in a rescue truck.

"The present system is so[...] we can live with," Roo[p said] "because the quality of ca[re is] good. It is adequate for thr[ee] calls a day, but certainly [as it] gets larger the need will ris[e."]

Although it would be p[...] only one paramedic to ha[...] Plano is assigning a tea[m to] ensure enough help is [...] needed.

"It really takes two [...] radio and do all [...] paramedic Danny McM[...] "It makes it so much [...]

easier."

"We can also double check each other," agreed his partner Jeff Amadon. "It increases the odds of our not making a mistake. If there's a question, we can discuss it and then [...]k the doctor."

[...] many things to see," [...] is almost

During their first month in action, paramedics in the Plano Fire Department have dealt with victims of a plane crash, car wrecks and medical emergencies. Doctors believe the paramedics have meant the difference in life and death to two heart attack patients. (Staff photo by Jana Beall).

FIRE
1980-1989
RESCUE

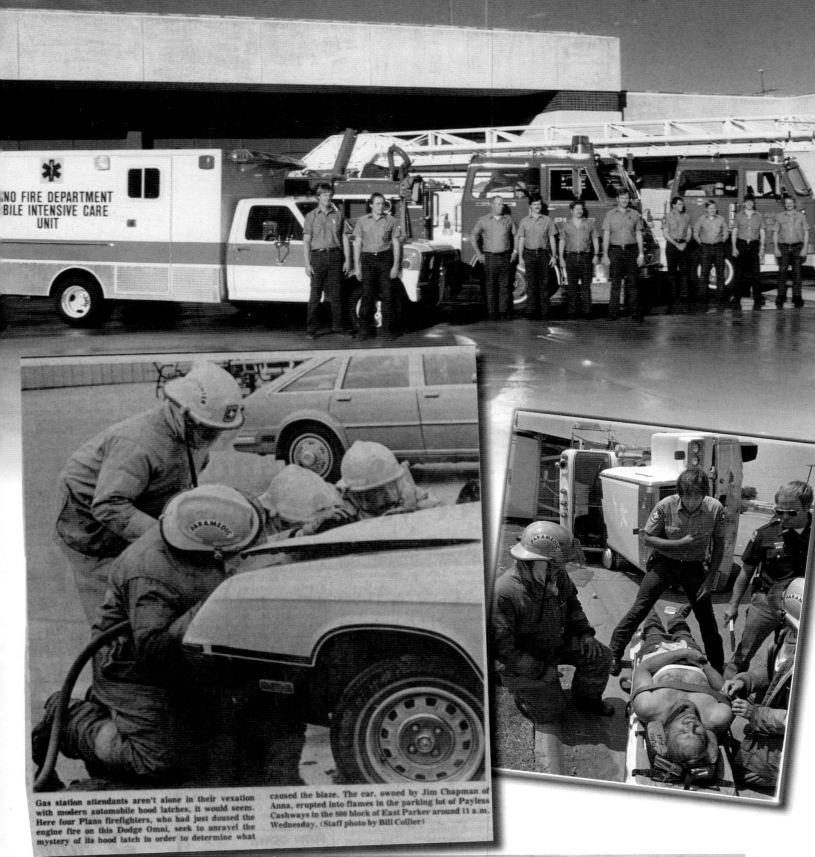

Gas station attendants aren't alone in their vexation with modern automobile hood latches, it would seem. Here four Plano firefighters, who had just doused the engine fire on this Dodge Omni, seek to unravel the mystery of its hood latch in order to determine what caused the blaze. The car, owned by Jim Chapman of Anna, erupted into flames in the parking lot of Payless Cashways in the 800 block of East Parker around 11 a.m. Wednesday. (Staff photo by Bill Collier)

—Plano Daily Star-Courier—Sunday, April 22, 1984

Texas weather means tornado weather

Skywarn spotters, sirens offer protection in Plano

By RICHARD LAGOW
Staff Writer

PLANO — They say that there is only one thing certain about Texas weather and that's nothing is for certain. And one of the great uncertainties of Texas weather is tornadoes.

Tornado season, in Texas, starts in mid-March and runs through April, May and June although tornadoes can and do occur at any time of the year.

City officials can use several methods to warn residents of an approaching tornado or other dangers, according to Plano Fire Marshal Bill Threet. Emergency warning sirens are located at all five Plano fire stations and a sixth will

save lives and reduce injuries."

The city also utilizes E-Alert radios in conjunction with local radio station KXVI-AM to communicate with residents.

The radios, available at Central Fire Station for $65, are tuned radio station KXVI in Plano.

"These radios can be activated automatically by an alert tone or you can listen to the radio as you normally do," Threet said.

Information that is transmitted by the radio is usually not more than 15 minutes old from the National Weather Service, according to Threet. By listening to the radio, residents can receive up-to-date information from local officials as well as area

New equipment

Jim Ticknor, a rescue expert and inventor, returned to Plano this week to train instructors in the use of the Ticknor Harness. The Plano Fire Department decided to purchase the harnesses after seeing a demonstration in February. The rescue device can be used from both high and low inaccessible locations. Training Officer Len Rush said the harness will be carried on apparatus for use in emergencies. The 12 men trained this week will hold additional schools until all firefighters can use the harnesses. (Staff photo by Jana Beall).

Dear Editor:

It has come to my attention that some fire stations in Plano, are totally closed down several days each week. Being a resident of Plano, I am very concerned that if a major fire (business or residence) were to happen, WHERE ARE THE FIREMEN?

I called central fire station to inquire about it and was told that the firemen were on inspections of nursing homes, businesses, etc....The representative assured me that there was nothing to worry about, but I am very concerned. After investigating, I found out the firemen are at some kind of class at Plano General Hospital and the town is only partially covered with a few firemen.

If any other citizens of Plano feel the way I do, please show your concern by calling the city of Plano, or the City Manager.

1983-

Name and address
withheld on request

87

Plano gets hazardous chemical squad

By CRAIG CLYNES
Staff Writer

PLANO — Because of the increasing number of accidents involving dangerous or hazardous substances, and because a large number of hazardous chemicals are used or stored in the city, the Plano Fire Department is developing a team which will be able to handle emergency situations where a dangerous chemical is involved.

"Because the deaths caused by hazardous materials are increasing, the fire department saw a need to develop its own hazardous materials team," says Captain Jack Pryor. Pryor, Lt. Ernest Roys and Capt. Carl Dane have been traveling to various conferences throughout the country gathering information on hazardous material (HazMat) teams in other fire departments.

What is a hazardous material? The fire department has come up with two definitions. The first is a substance or material, which by its form or quantity, poses danger to health and property when commercially transported.

The second is any element, compound or combination of the two which is flammable or corrosive and by its storage, handling, processing or packaging may have bad effects on people and the environment.

In a report to the city proposing a HazMat team, Lt. Roys indicates 11 of the top 25 chemicals manufactured in this country and identified as hazardous by the Department of Transportation are used or stored in Plano. The report also says all 25 hazardous chemicals are shipped by railroad companies which own tracks within the city limits.

In addition, Roys estimates there are 5,000 new chemicals invented each year. Some are documented as dangerous, while others are never written about. "Who is to say an unknown chemical is not going to travel through Plano," Roys adds.

The report also says the railroads and thoroughfares through the city have the potential for a chemical accident or spill. It adds the Department of Transportation acknowledges 50,000 truck companies, railroads and airlines haul hazardous materials.

"Any city the size of Plano with railroads and thoroughfares must have a HazMat program," Roys says.

Pryor says the fire service became involved in hazardous materials because it usually is the department asked to help take charge of program...

Plano firefighter Mike Shafer, dressed in his protective suit, opens the hazardous material response kit. The suit, response kit, and other items in the... ment has been gather... ...e HazMat teams to help it create a well-trained... ...in Plano. The department hopes to ... ...end of the year. (Staff photo by...)

Plano firefighters Stan Hamm and Calvin Cook display equipment for handling hazardous chemical spills.
Steve Knaps/Dallas Times He...

PLANO
Team trained to handle chemical accidents

By PAM TROBOY
Staff Writer

3-12-86

Saying a hazardous chemical spill is "waiting to happen" in Plano, fire officials have formed a highly trained 21-member clean up team and bought special equipment to handle accidents.

The team, stationed at the Spring Creek Parkway fire station, will complete a 230-hour training program Mar 1 on the varieties and characteristics of hundreds of chemicals. Additional training will be provided by companies that use or store chemi...

Fire Capt. Ernest Roys, who is teaching the course, said officials have determined that 11 of the 25 most common hazardous chemicals are stored in or transported through Plano. He said that in the Dallas area, Fort Worth has a chemical spill team and Dallas is forming such a unit.

Although there has not been a chemical spill in Plano, Roys believes its only a matter of time before an accident occurs.

...have that many chemicals and the ...traffic problems are get... ...to assume an incident is ...pen," he said.

The first appropriation for the team $24,000, was made last September, he said.

The department has purchased reference books on industrial chemicals, a patching system to fill holes in tank cars and pipes, protective gear and other equipment. It also purchased a new pumper truck with devices used to dispense dry chemicals and foam, which are used to contain spilled chemicals.

Money for more equipment will be requested in next year's budget, Roys said. To save expenses, Plano officials are negotiating with nearby cities to form a regional spill team.

FIRE 1980-1989 RESCUE

1985	The first Haz-Mat program and team are introduced
1985	The Mayfield-Russell Fire Training Center is dedicated May 31 honoring former Fire Chiefs Lee Mayfield (Plano) and Richard Russell (Richardson)
1985	*Learn Not to Burn* is introduced into Plano Independent School District curriculum grades 1 – 5 in September
1985	Department receives 3 new 8-passenger E1 pumper enclosed cab engines with heating and air in November. These are the first vehicles of this type put into service in Texas
1986	Station 6 opens at 900 Seabrook Drive
1986	City's first mobile public safety command post is introduced in June, a 1985 18-foot Chevy step van
1986	$16,000 is raised by Plano firefighters for the Jerry Lewis muscular dystrophy Labor Day telethon

VOL. 98—NO. 184 PLANO, TEXAS   1 SECTION   16 PAGES   TWENTY FIVE CEN

Recruit school offers multifaceted training for Plano firefighters

3-5-86

Editor's note: This is the last in a   Plano recruits learn about spectors.

Wednesda...

New firefighters

The members of the Plano Fire Department's recently completed Recruit School line up just after graduation ceremonies were held last Friday in City Hall. Of the 21 men in the class, 17 will work with the Plano Fire Department, three will go to the Allen Fire Department and one will go to the McKinney Fire Department. Members of the class are Clay Hooten, Bill Hawley, Randy Jones, Wayne York, Dan Burks, Danny Decker, John Cardwell, Jim Pe... Glenn Pressley, Ernest McCoy, Mark Barnett, Mike Malone, Mark Sh... Bill Boyette, Mark Baker, Jason Collier, Bruce Cook, Don McKinney, Ru... Reynolds, Mike Ussery and Scott Thompson. (Staff photo by Scott Nowli...

1986 Station 6

FIRE
1980-1989
RESCUE

Capt. Kirk Owen

Firefighter teaches city to 'learn not to burn'

Captain Kirk Owen of the Plano Fire Department, right, instructs firefighter John Cardwell about the Learn Not To Burn program.

Scott Nowling/Staff photo

By BUCK WARGO
Staff Writer

Helping children and the public learn about fire prevention is one reason Kirk Owen says he enjoys his work.

Owen, the media information officer for the Plano Fire Department, is responsible for training firefighters and PISD teachers to teach school children the "Learn Not To Burn" program.

"The teachers and the firefighters are the key for the fire safety program functioning," Owen said.

"The program is important because through education we can prevent injuries and deaths resulting from fires."

The Dallas-born Owen, 34, has been with the fire department for seven years. He has spent the last two years in his current position setting up and operating the program.

He started as a firefighter and has now worked his way to the level of captain.

"It is different being a staff officer. The captains in the stations are responsible for their men and the station. I am managing and coordinating a program," he said.

Owen says he enjoyed working in the stations.

"To be perfectly honest, I miss the comradarie of working with a bunch of guys. I miss the exhilaration of responding to an emergency and handling it right then," he said.

Owen says that ability to give

Today's Spotlight

instant assistance is the big difference between working in the station and in the office.

"In a fire station . . . ideally and an em . . . oriented. The . . . the fire ou . . . one out . . . them. Y . . . right av . . . ments . . .

position, I am looking at long-term results and things that are less tangible," he said.

Owen says it is hard to tell how much an impact the program is having.

"It is really tough to say this particular program caused these numbers. You just look at numbers and think if there is a decrease the program helped in some way," he . . .

. . . it is a never-. . . tion, he . . . with . . .

"At some point shortly after Chief Peterson came to Plano he asked me to start a public fire safety education program. We had been doing fire stations tours and schools visits showing off our trucks but we didn't have a true fire safety education program. This fire extinguisher class was one of our early public education efforts. Our programs were based on, and dependent on, companies assisting or delivering the presentations we developed. With their help and support we were able to build a very good fire safety education program, which even included Plano Independent School District writing fire safety topics into their curriculum."

- Kirk Owen,
Assistant Chief, Retired

Group of Apparatus & Personnel 1985

Fire Department to expand operations in 1982

Sunday, February 28, 1982—Plano Daily Star-Co

Paramedic training to begin, new west side stations planned

PLANO—The Fire Department will begin basic paramedic service this spring.

Three firefighters have completed training and will be assigned to the rescue truck housed at Central Station as soon as necessary equipment arrives.

Additional personnel will take the 16-course at Southwestern Medical School this to ensure a paramedic always on duty.

The program is phased in because cost. The first year cost almost $1 much of it due to the of personnel training.

The paramedic work under

"first responder" in Drive and 6000 Rour west Plano.

All ambulances are staffed with emergency medical technician who can provide cardiopulmonary resuscitation, bandage and splint, administer oxygen, take vital signs, do traction and deliver

Wooden shingles a firefighter's nightmare

Homes with wooden shingles destroyed by fire

Fire chief recommends treatment for shingles

built to class "C" roofing specifica-

Fireworks...

Officials warn against illegal, careless use

By PAM THROOY
Staff Writer

The Fourth of July has traditionally been the time for

because of the illegal and careless use of fireworks.

FRIDAY, JANUARY 11, 1985

Helping in an emergency

Paramedics, emergency medical technicians provide quality care in critical situations

City employs EMS coordinator

Klein hopes to modernize, improve education

By CRAIG CLYNES
Staff Writer

PLANO — For Ken Klein there's no reason Plano can not have the best emergency medical service in the area. Klein is the city's new emergency medical service (EMS) coordinator and he hopes to improve the present system to accomplish that goal.

"There is no reason why Plano can't be a leader in the fire/EMS services in the future," said Klein, who started in his new position this past Monday.

Klein said the job opened up because growth has caused the city to hire someone to coordinate the EMS system full time. "It is no longer feasible for the fire department to try to keep up with the EMS systems on a part-time basis," he said.

Even though Klein assessed the fire department and current EMS system as excellent, there are some goals he would like to accomplish to

Ken Klein, Plano's new EMS coordinator, would like to see the public better educated about EMS services, especially in the area of cardiopulminary resuscitation (CPR).

modernize the system. He described one of them.

"We hope to have advanced life support equipment and paramedic companies at every fire station," Klein said. Fire stations three and five already have paramedic engine companies in use.

Another goal is to continue education for both paramedics and firefighters in EMS. "The state has a requirement that paramedics and EMT's need a certain amount of hours in continuing education," Klein said. He added paramedics have to be recertified every four years, so a continuing education program could help them.

Besides educating the fire department employees, Klein hopes to improve public awareness in emergency medical attention. He said the department is thinking of starting public classes in the area of cardiopulmonary resuscitation (CPR). Klein feels this class is very important. "Every family should

have someone trained to do CPR," he said.

He has a special reason for emphasizing the CPR classes. "If a person begins CPR on a heart attack victim before the paramedics can reach him, we can expect the survival rate to be higher than without CPR," Klein said.

He hopes to work with other institutions, especially Plano General Hospital, in developing classes for both the fire department and the public.

The fire department now has 41 paramedics in its staff, but Klein said all fire department personnel are trained as emergency medical technicians (EMT). "This means every firefighter is capable of giving basic life support service," Klein said. A paramedic is trained to give advanced life support help.

As EMS coordinator, Klein's basic duties will be administrative. He will prepare the budget for the EMS

Continued on page 3

Since starting his new job Monday, Ken Klein has been busy organizing his files before meeting the fire department's paramedics. Klein is the new EMS coordinator for the city. (Staff photos).

93

Jaws of Life

Plano Fire Department workers had to use the Jaws of Life to cut their way into this automobile to rescue Ruth Carr, a traffic accident victim, Wednesday at about 3:30 p.m. Carr was transported to Plano General Hospital following the automobile accident which occurred at the intersection of Woodburn Corners and Park Blvd. (Staff photo by Scott Nowling).

Night Shot of Central Bays

Firefighters adjust to 'no standing' policy

Some firefighters oppose mandate

By LINDA CARRICO
Staff Writer

Friday, September 18, 1987

Kayla Nossaman/Staff artist

Plano residents no longer will see firefighters standing on rear bumpers or jump seats of emergency vehicles as they race to and from fire and accident scenes around the city.

Fire Chief Bill Peterson has eliminated the practices long associated with fire service, and now requires firefighters to be seated in all emergency vehicles and secured by seat belts.

"They are archaic traditions that do not provide for the safety of firefighters," Peterson said, noting that 20 percent of the 120 firefighters killed annually on the job occur

Turn to POLICY, page 4A

1980-1989

FIRE RESCUE

1987 — Second aerial ladder truck acquired; housed at Central Fire Station

1987 — Emergency 911 telephone service is established in the GTE service area of Plano

1987 — Lt. Bob Manley named as *Firefighter of the Year* March 8 as new annual award is unveiled

1987 — Department among first in nation to purchase Computer Aided Management Equipment software for emergency operations

1987 — *Learn Not to Burn* hot air balloon purchased in September, piloted by Chief William E. Peterson

1987 — No bumper or jump seat standing policy mandated effective September 18. All must be seated, secured with seatbelts.

1988 — Station 7 opens at 5602 Democracy Drive

1988 — Fire Department Chaplaincy begun

1988 — Fire Explorer Post #215 formed

1988 — Teddy Bear *Bear-A-Medics* stocked on ambulances beginning in March to soothe treated children

Fire Cat

Firefighter's Pecan Pie

1 cup light corn syrup
3 slightly beaten eggs
1 teaspoon vanilla extract
Pinch or two of salt
1 cup white sugar
1 cup pecans (whole or chopped,
  either way is fine)
1 unbaked pie crust

Mix the syrup, eggs, vanilla, salt, sugar and pecans and then pour the mix into the pie crust. Bake at 350° for about 45 minutes or until the center is set.

Bearing up in emergencies

Plano ambulances stocked with teddy bears for hurt, sick children

By Megan Doren
Staff Writer

Beginning this week, injured children who have to ride in an ambulance will get a new friend to take home.

The city of Plano's three ambulances have been stocked with 350 stuffed bears to be given to children ages 3 to 9 who are treated by paramedics.

A Plano firefighter attending the National Fire Academy in Emmitsburg, Md., heard about a program in Sandy City, Utah, that gave the stuffed toys to injured children in conjunction with the city's trauma unit, said Plano Fire Chief William Peterson.

"The bears comforted and calmed the children in a normally traumatic situation," Peterson said. "In a time that is both confusing and scary for the kids, the bears take their attention off what is going on around them, which enables the paramedics to communicate with them."

The "Bear-A-Medics" were donated to the Plano Fire Department by GTE Southwest to promote the program and the city's 911 emergency phone system.

The 9-inch brown-and-white bears sport a blue-and-white T-shirt that has "Plano Fire Department, Call 911 Emergency" printed on the front and the GTE logo on the back.

The number of bears, 350, was established because the department estimates that is how many children in that age group will be treated by paramedics in a 12-month period.

The department estimates it will answer 4,200 ambulance calls this year.

The Dallas Morning News: Judy Walgren

Chris Bechtold, 21, a firefighter at Plano fire station No. 3, holds one of the new "Bear-A-Medics" that will be carried on city ambulances and given to hurt or sick children.

FIRE
1980-1989
RESCUE

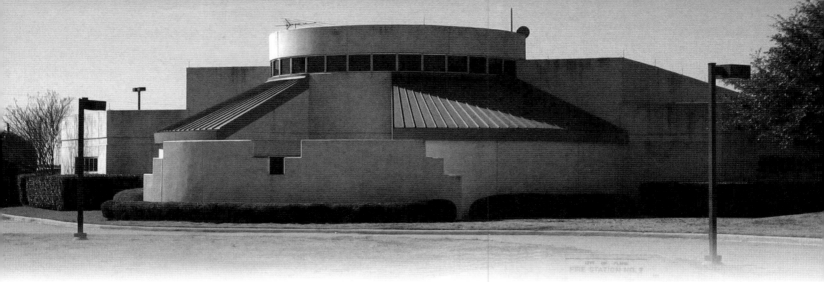

1988 Station 7

"I later moved into the newest addition which was Fire Station 7. About all we had were Frito Lay, EDS, the new JC Penney, and Southland Life. Daytime district population was around 15,000 but nighttime consisted of about 30 janitors."

- Carl Dane,
Captain, Retired

HELP
YOUR
FIRE
FIGHTER
FIGHT
MUSCULAR DYSTROPHY

SUPPORT THE

FIRE
FIGHTERS
CRUSADE

DEFEAT
MUSCLE
DISEASES

HELP
YOUR
FIRE
FIGHTER
FIGHT
MUSCULAR DYSTROPHY

Assistant Fire Chief Bob Acker shows off Plano's new pride and joy, the Public Safety Command Post. The 18-foot Chevrolet step van will be used by the city in emergency situations. The van contains a variety of communications devices which enables it to serve as the nerve center of field operatio

"In the early 1980's, the Plano Fire Department began moving to more formal incident management. Following initial training in the Fireground Command System by Chief Brunacini of the Phoenix Fire Department, we realized that we needed to have a fixed Command Post that could deploy for larger and longer duration accidents. Funding was tough in those days, but the vehicle was acquired and outfitted by fire personnel. Former firefighter Jerry Temple constructed the interior of the structure including partitions, overhead cabinets, work desks and the like. Other firefighters helped with installing lights, marker boards, and other fixtures. The final touch was the installation of a number of different radio systems which allowed communication with all area Police and Fire public safety agencies on a variety of different bands and frequencies. The Mobile Command Post also served as a backup for the PFD dispatchers and later the Public Safety Communications functions."

–Bob Acker,
Assistant Chief, Retired

1/18/88   1) IN SERVICE AT 3's AT 0630 HRS.
2) FUEL, WATER OKAY
   OIL ½ QRT LOW, LIGHTS & EQUIPMENT
   PRESENT AND WORKING
3) CLEARANCE LIGHT ON TOP, REAR OF
   BOX MISSING RED COVER
4) DRUG INVENTORY COMPLETED
5) PORTABLE RECHARGED
6) ADDED 9 GAL. FUEL 2100 HRS

"I am the mash'd fireman with breast-bone broken,
tumbling walls buried me in their debris.
Heat and smoke I inspired,
I heard the yelling shouts of my comrades,
I heard the distant click of their picks and shovels.
They have clear'd the beams away,
they tenderly lift me forth."

- *Song of Myself,*
Walt Whitman,
1819-1892

"I remember changing from long cotton bunker coats and tall rubber boots to Nomex coats and pants. It was after Craig McMillan and Glen Taylor were seriously burned during a house fire. Chief Peterson went to the Council and got the whole Department new protective clothing. This was just one of so many improvements in safety, protective clothing, and equipment. A few years later, Chief Caldwell upgraded us to PBI outer shells for our protective clothing. SCBA, gloves, helmets, hose, nozzles, apparatus and everything else was always improving."

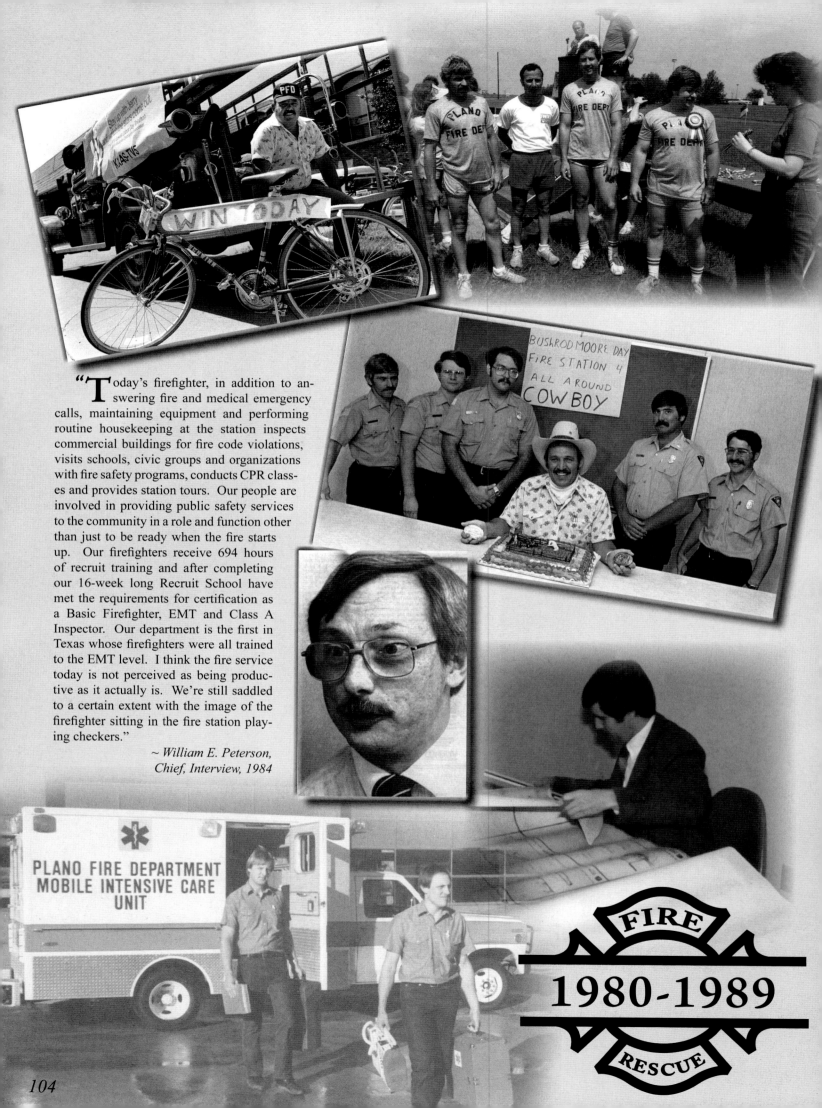

"Today's firefighter, in addition to answering fire and medical emergency calls, maintaining equipment and performing routine housekeeping at the station inspects commercial buildings for fire code violations, visits schools, civic groups and organizations with fire safety programs, conducts CPR classes and provides station tours. Our people are involved in providing public safety services to the community in a role and function other than just to be ready when the fire starts up. Our firefighters receive 694 hours of recruit training and after completing our 16-week long Recruit School have met the requirements for certification as a Basic Firefighter, EMT and Class A Inspector. Our department is the first in Texas whose firefighters were all trained to the EMT level. I think the fire service today is not perceived as being productive as it actually is. We're still saddled to a certain extent with the image of the firefighter sitting in the fire station playing checkers."

~ *William E. Peterson,*
Chief, Interview, 1984

Auditorium fire closes Williams High

Second fire empties high school

TUESDAY, FEBRUARY 26, 1985

By GREG GALLIER
Staff Writer

PLANO — For the second time in less than one week, students and staff at Williams High School were evacuated yesterday when fire broke out in the building.

contained within that area by firefighters. The first engine arrived on the scene at approximately 9:45 a.m.

The fire was extinguished within 15 minutes, according to Fire Chief Bill Peterson, who estimated the

'We are proceeding under the assumption that this fire was purposely set.'
— Supt. H. Wayne Hendrick

The school's football stadium again served as temporary residence for students, who remained there for some two hours before being herded back inside around noon for the resumption of regularly scheduled classes.

Monday's blaze began in a custodian's supply closet and was

damage to be between $10,000 and $15,000.

While the cause of last week's fire at Williams is still under investigation, Peterson called the origin of yesterday's blaze "suspicious" in nature.

That assessment was mirrored by

Continued on page

FIRE
1990-1999
RESCUE

1990 Plano population: 128,713

1990 Ross Perot's EDS facility and JCPenney begin construction on new world headquarter locations in Perot's exclusive corporate campus park – Legacy

1991 Department reorganizes into major divisions: Administration, Operations, Support Services, Personnel Services, Fire Prevention

1992 Motorola 800MHz trunked radio system enables Fire and Police dispatch operations to merge to form the Communications Department, centralized at Municipal Center

1993 End of year reports show department responded to 7,678 calls in 1992, an increase from 7,171 responded calls in 1991

1993 Truck companies are equipped to provide Advanced Life Support and become Paramedic Truck Companies

1994 Station 8 opens at 4555 Hedgcoxe Road

1994 Station 1 and Fire Administration open at 1901 K Avenue, ending the final chapter of Fire and City Hall sharing joint facilities

1995 *Sparky* hot air balloon replaces *Learn Not to Burn* balloon

1995 Fire affects 22 homes in Whiffletree subdivision in October resulting in Plano banning HOA's from requiring wood shingle roofs

1995 Plano Fire Department holds first Citizen's Fire Academy class

1996 *Sparky the Fire Dog* becomes PFD's official mascot, replacing *Fire Cat*

1998 Station 9 opens at 6625 W. Parker Road

1998 Plano Fire Department earns Class 1 Public Protection Classification from ISO, the first Texas city to attain this rating

1999 Station No. 10 Opens at 3540 McDermott Road

1999 George Bush Turnpike Opens for Plano service July 2

Plano Fire, Emergency Calls

Category	1991	1990	Percent increase
Number of fires	744	672	6.8
Property damage	$2.645 million	$3.123 million	
Injuries (fire)	22	30	
Rescue, EMS calls	4,123	3,836	

Saturday, March 21, 1992 — Plano Star Courie

Emergency assistance calls rise

By KERI GOINS
Staff writer

The number of fire calls and other emergency incidents requiring assistance from the Plano Fire Department increased 6.8 percent in 1991, compared to the same period of 1990.

The department responded to 7,337 calls in 1991; 6,870 in 1990.

Fire department spokesman Bill Jones said the department considered the increase slight, and noted that it had been about the same the last four or five years.

"From about 1986, which time we started keeping clos amount of calls, up to now the i remained steady with approxim 13 percent rise each year," Jo

Overall, figures for 1991 w 1990, with only a few noticea such as in the category of ot incidents, which includes car fir and trash fires.

The number of trash fires ro

Turn to C

Fire blamed on child playing with matches

A 6-year-old boy playing with matches set a mattress on fire in an apartment in the 1300 block of Rigsbee Drive Saturday morning, fire investigators said.

According to fire officials, a babysitter evacuated five children from the apartment when the mattress caught fire at about 1:10 a.m. Firefighters doused the blaze before it spread, fire officials said.

Damage was estimated at $50 and no injuries were reported.

Plano police are conducting an investigation into possible child endangerment due to the "terrible conditions of the apartment," fire officials said. The apartment was in disarray and living conditions were poor, officials said.

1994 Station 1

Brush Truck

FP Van

Ford Explorer

108

1996 Apparatus and Personnel

Suburban

DIAL 911 EMERGENCY   PLANO FIRE-RESCUE

City will purchase new ladder fire truck

The Plano City Council approved the emergency purchase of an aerial ladder fire truck in the wake of the collision of two fire trucks at the intersection of Avenue K and East 15th Street last month. An engine truck broadsided a ladder truck while both vehicles were in the process of responding to separate emergency calls.

While the damage to the ladder truck will probably amount to $50,000, the five months it will take to repair the 1992 model at a Wisconsin factory necessitated the early purchase of another truck at a cost of $430,395 from the city's equipment replacement fund, according to Fire Chief Bill Peterson.

While approval was granted last October to replace a 1982 model, the city was in the process of taking bids on a new truck when the accident occurred, Peterson said. The fire department will continue to use the 1982 model fire truck while the newer model is out, he said.

PLANO FIRE-RESCUE

Stats show careless cooking leading cause of kitchen fires

By TIM PARETI
Staff writer

As the old saying goes, they never _____ happen to them.

reported injuries, 11 deaths and $3.1 million in pr____ _____mage."

In Plano _____ reported k_____ $381,711 _____ majority c _____ the stov_____ me. T_____ arted _____ tchen_____ "The_____ed t_____ r c_____

Kitchen Fires	1990	1991
Total	50	60
*Loss	$507	$382
Single-family	38	47
Duplex	2	1
Apartments	10	12
Cooking equipment		
Stove top	25	35
Oven	6	5
Other	7	4
No equipment	11	14
Non-cooking equip	1	2
Ignition factor		
Misuse of heat	5	8
Discarded material	6	8
Kids playing with fire	1	5
Misuse of ignited mtrl.	7	6
Mechanical failure	1	7
Design deficiency	1	1
Operational deficiency	0	7
Leaving unattended	29	22
Undetermined	0	3

FIRE
1990-1999
RESCUE

1994 Station 8

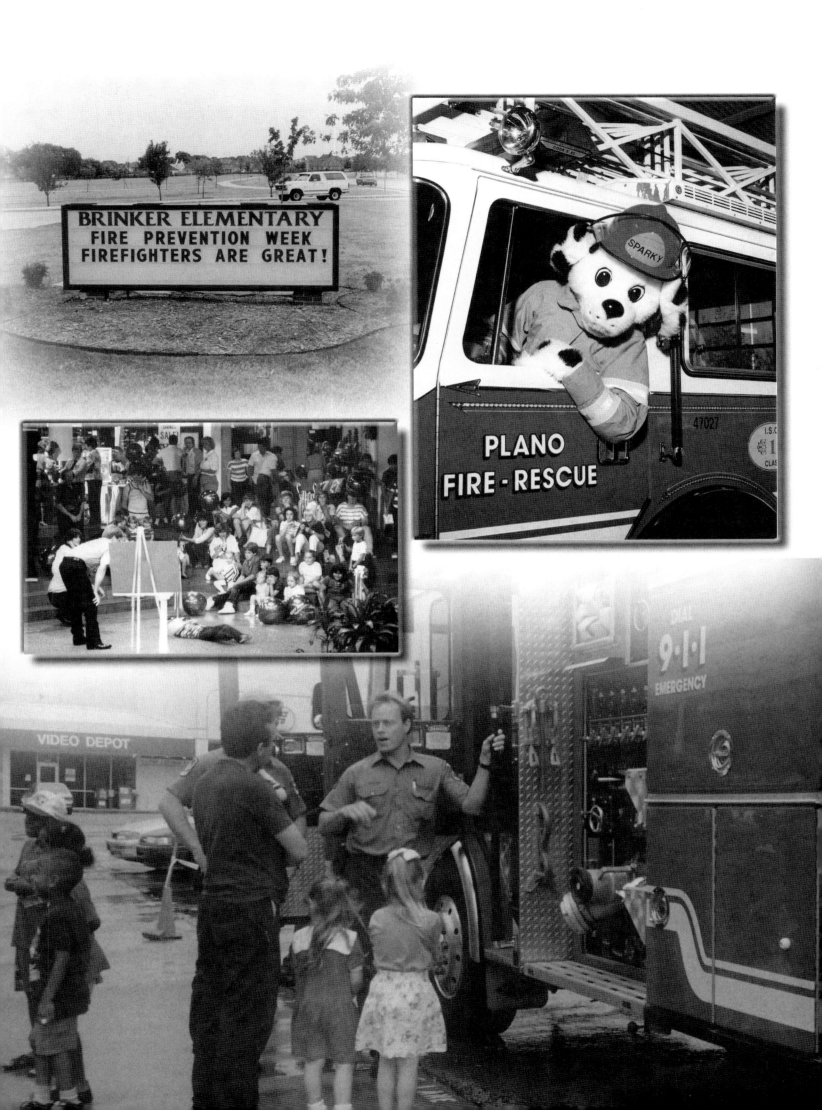

BRINKER ELEMENTARY
FIRE PREVENTION WEEK
FIREFIGHTERS ARE GREAT!

PLANO
FIRE - RESCUE

SPARKY

47027

VIDEO DEPOT

DIAL
9·1·1
EMERGENCY

Firefighters face tougher certification requirments

By KERI GOINS
Staff writer

The task of becoming a Plano firefighter was made more difficult Tuesday with the Civil Service Commission's adoption of stricter requirements for those desiring to take the entry-level exam.

Although several firefighters voiced concerns that the new requirements may discriminate against minorities, the commission voted unanimously to approve the eligibility changes.

Previously, the only requirements for the exam were a minimum age of 18 and a high school education. Under the guidelines adopted, certification by the Texas Fire Commission or equivalent training is required.

After review, City Attorney Gary Chatham determined the proposal is legal.

Plano Fire Chief Bill Peterson said the plan will save the city more than $155,000 in test administration fees

alone, which in turn will save taxpayers money.

"Last time we gave the test, 900 applicants showed up to take it for only 20 to 30 openings. With the new certification requirement, only about 150 applicants are expected to take the test," Peterson said.

He said the guidelines will help weed out the people who are not serious about becoming firefighters.

"We waste a lot of time and money by having to give the test to people who are only thinking about being a firefighter because they heard it might be fun or because their friend is one," Peterson said.

The only places in Collin County offering certification classes are Collin County Community College and Frisco Fire Department.

The CCCC program is given once a year and consists of two semesters (18 hours) for $1,203.

"I definitely think this proposal will discriminate against people of

Turn to CIVIL, Page 6A

1998 Station 9

This is my job...

This is my job...

MEET BILL JONES, assistant program analyst and operations supervisor of communications for the fire department. Bill has been with the PFD for 13 years. Prior to assuming his present post, Bill was a fireman for 11 years. "I wanted to be a fireman because my father was a fireman. That's all I ever knew." Bill's father retired from the Richardson FD with 23 years service and a total of 46 years in the fire service. As Operations Supervisor, Bill is responsible for overseeing the day to day operations of the Communications Division. "I'm on special assignment to the administrative staff," he says. "Basically, what I started out doing was video and audio coordination. I took pictures of the prepared slides and worked with TeleCable." The dispatchers are all located at Central Fire Station. "We receive all the calls for help and keep track of the equipment in the city to see what's available to..." an emergency. We're the communic... the public and fire stations," he ex... likes his job because of the respon... a challenge in what it boiled dow... shift for years and my wife and ... decided it would be nice for m... [...]king. Despite the [...]

MEET VIRGINIA ALLMAN, administrative secretary at the Plano Fire Department. Prior to joining the PFD administrative staff, Virginia worked as a secretary in personnel for the City of Plano for four years. She was promoted to her present position over a year ago. As administrative secretary, Virginia's main responsibility is to provide secretarial support for both... Peterson and Assistant... mission to her... a real challenge." But Virginia never backs away from a challenge. "She does the work of two people," Chief Peterson says. "But I do think she likes to see me go out of town so she can catch up!" he jokes. In addition to keeping her bosses and the rest of the staff on schedule, Virginia makes sure all communication flows smoothly between other city departments. "It seems some days I know too many things that are happening and other days I don't know enough," she laughs. Virginia and her husband Alton have lived in Plano since 1950. They have four grown children. In her spare time, Virginia enjoys puttering around her house. She can often be found in the kitchen, whipping up family dinners. "I really enjoy cooking for my family," she confesses. (By Trisha Wheeler. Staff photo by Scott Nowling)

1999 Station 10

Sabu puts his nose to the grindstone

K-9 Response Team new to department

By KERI GOINS
Staff writer

The city's newest recruit in the fire department weighs only 65 pounds.

The services he is able to offer Plano, however, are only available at one other fire fighting agency in the state.

His name is Sabu and his job is to sniff out accelerants at fire sites investigators deem as suspicious in nature.

The 2-year-old black Labrador Retriever and his handler, firefighter paramedic Andrew Rohde, make up the department's new K-9 Response Team, which is funded through a state grant and

Turn to K-9, Page 12A

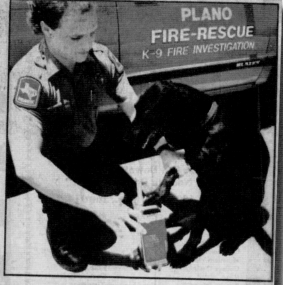

Ian Halperin/Staff photo

Plano firefighter Andrew Rohde and Sabu are Plano's newest team in fire investigation. Sabu, who is trained to recognize 11 different accelerants, is the only one of his kind in the Metroplex. The K-9 Response Team has already helped to make the arrest in four arson cases in its ___

Store fire ruled arson

Thursday, June 17, 1993 — Plano Star Courier

Brook Mays damage at $1 million

By TIM PARETI
Staff writer

A Wednesday morning fire destroyed a Plano music store, causing an estimated $1 million in damages.

Brook Mays Music Store, 1729 Central Expressway, was razed in the 12:45 a.m. blaze.

Plano fire officials ruled the fire an arson.

According to Plano Fire Marshal Russ Mower, the fire started in the northwest corner of the building when roofing material on the ground was ignited. The fire spread to the roof and burned most of the building, he said.

Firefighters fought the blaze for about an hour and finished cleanup around 8 a.m. Wednesday.

"This fire appears to be along the lines of vandalism," Mower said.

Fire officials are still investigating to determine what was used to ignite the roofing material, Mower said.

No arrests had been made Wednesday in connection with the fire.

Music literature and numerous musical instruments — including guitars, drum sets, pianos and orchestra equipment — were ruined in the fire.

According to Larry Tucker, director of performing arts for Plano Independent School District, hundreds of pieces of PISD

Plano 1995

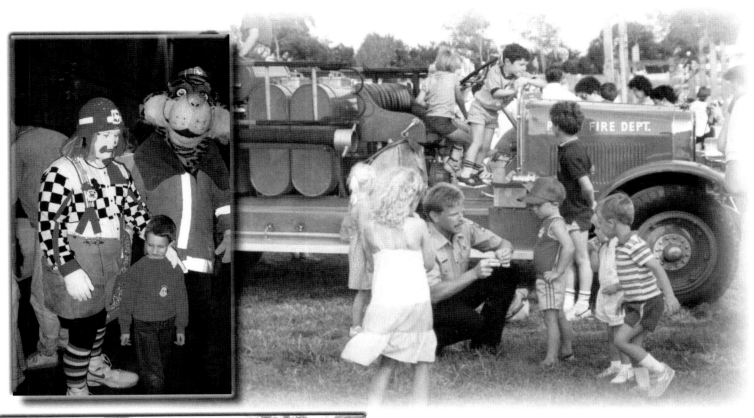

117

Plano Star Courier — Saturday, June 26, 1993

Fire engines collide

Fire investigators inspect the damage after two Plano fire engines collided Friday afternoon at the intersection of Avenue K and 15th Street. According to Division Fire Chief Bob Acker, an engine traveling eastbound on 15th Street when it broadsided a ladder truck that was traveling northbound on Avenue K. Both fire vehicles were responding to separate emergency calls at the time of the collision. There were no injuries. The damage amount has not yet been determined.

Walter Granberry/Staff

FIRE
1990-1999
RESCUE

"Joining the Plano Fire Department Explorer Post 215 was one of the best decisions I ever made. It's the foundation on which my career has been built. The mentorship and training offered by the post rivaled that of actual training academies. Not only was I exposed to the life of a firefighter, but I was allowed to participate and train like one. I was lucky enough to get assigned to Station 8 on A shift. They were not only mentors - they were my friends. I was always humbled and honored when they called me a member of the crew. I stayed in touch with the crew throughout college and after graduating continued on to fire academy and paramedic school. I was finally eligible to take the most important test of my life and was able to enter and make it through Plano's hiring process. It was a surreal experience to put on a real Plano Fire Department 'blue polo' uniform for the first time. Even more exciting is working next to and with personnel that I looked up to as an explorer in my 'grey polo.' I continue to pinch myself every day that I was able to achieve my dream. I continue to dream and set goals, knowing that anything is possible as a member of Plano Fire Rescue."

~ *Justin Samuel, Fire Rescue Specialist*

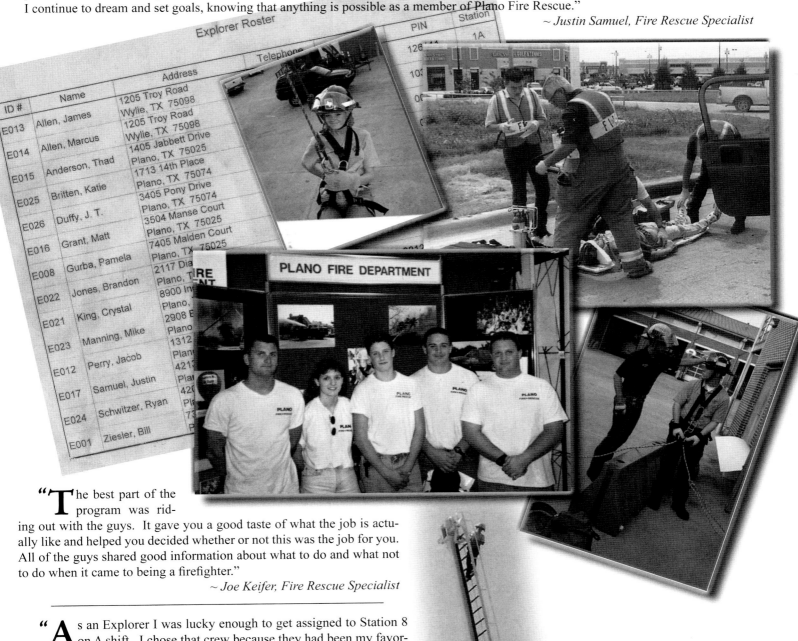

ID #	Name	Address
E013	Allen, James	1205 Troy Road, Wylie, TX 75098
E014	Allen, Marcus	1205 Troy Road, Wylie, TX 75098
E015	Anderson, Thad	1405 Jabbett Drive, Plano, TX 75025
E025	Britten, Katie	1713 14th Place, Plano, TX 75074
E026	Duffy, J. T.	3405 Pony Drive, Plano, TX 75074
E016	Grant, Matt	3504 Manse Court, Plano, TX 75025
E008	Gurba, Pamela	7405 Malden Court, Plano, TX 75025
E022	Jones, Brandon	2117 Dia... Plano,...
E021	King, Crystal	8900 In... Plano,...
E023	Manning, Mike	2908 E... Plano...
E012	Perry, Jacob	1312... Plan...
E017	Samuel, Justin	421... Pla...
E024	Schwitzer, Ryan	420... Pl...
E001	Ziesler, Bill	73... P...

"The best part of the program was riding out with the guys. It gave you a good taste of what the job is actually like and helped you decided whether or not this was the job for you. All of the guys shared good information about what to do and what not to do when it came to being a firefighter."

~ *Joe Keifer, Fire Rescue Specialist*

"As an Explorer I was lucky enough to get assigned to Station 8 on A shift. I chose that crew because they had been my favorite during my ride outs in Citizens Fire Academy. A lot of my fellow Explorers gave me grief because I chose a "slow station." Truth is, I picked one of the best crews, and got to see a lot of really good calls. They were not only mentors, but they were my friends. I was always humbled and honored when they called me a member of the crew. Personnel came and went, but the solid group was the following:

Captain Dennis Moore
FAO Ron Cooper
FRS Chris Patterson
FRS Kenny Braley
FRS Kevin Dritschler
FRS Trish Swavey
FRS Art Lujan
FRS Ron Robertson
(Ranks as of my assignment there from 1998-2004)."

~ *Justin Samuel, Fire Rescue Specialist*

119

HAPPY
40TH
TO
CHIEF Bubba
CALDWELL

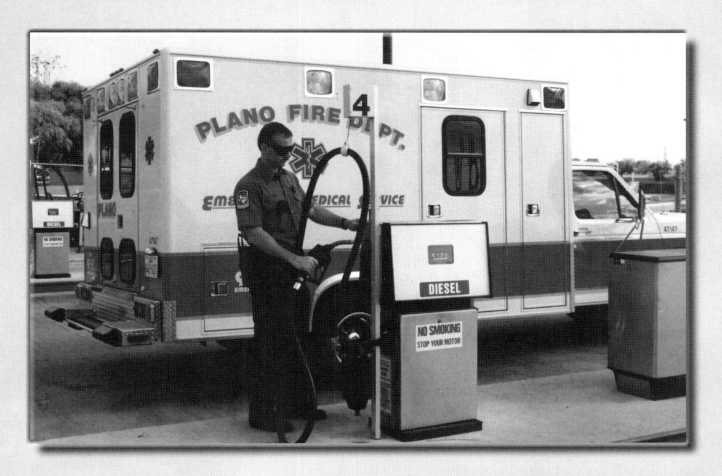

"**I** grew up with RESCUE 8 and EMERGENCY on television. The stories were always interesting. I also grew up in a volunteer fire department town. Being a small town (in the 1950s and 60s) we knew everybody who was a member. You saw the progression of paramedics becoming a part of the department and the volunteers going away. When Plano offered the Citizens Fire Academy years ago, I thought that would be interesting to see closer-up at the workings of a department. I was impressed with what the department did compared to the 'normal' life of the TV departments. Their friendliness and acceptance of people kept me interested so much that I ended up getting involved with Fire Dispatch, Operations and ultimately hiring on with Dallas Fire Rescue."

--Rob Johnson,
Plano Citizen and graduate of
Citizens Fire Academy Class 7

FIRE

1990-1999

RESCUE

"**I** was surprised by the number of hands-on activities that allowed me to perform some of the duties of firemen in a safe and controlled environment."

--John McGraw,
Plano Citizen and graduate of
Citizens Fire Academy Class 32

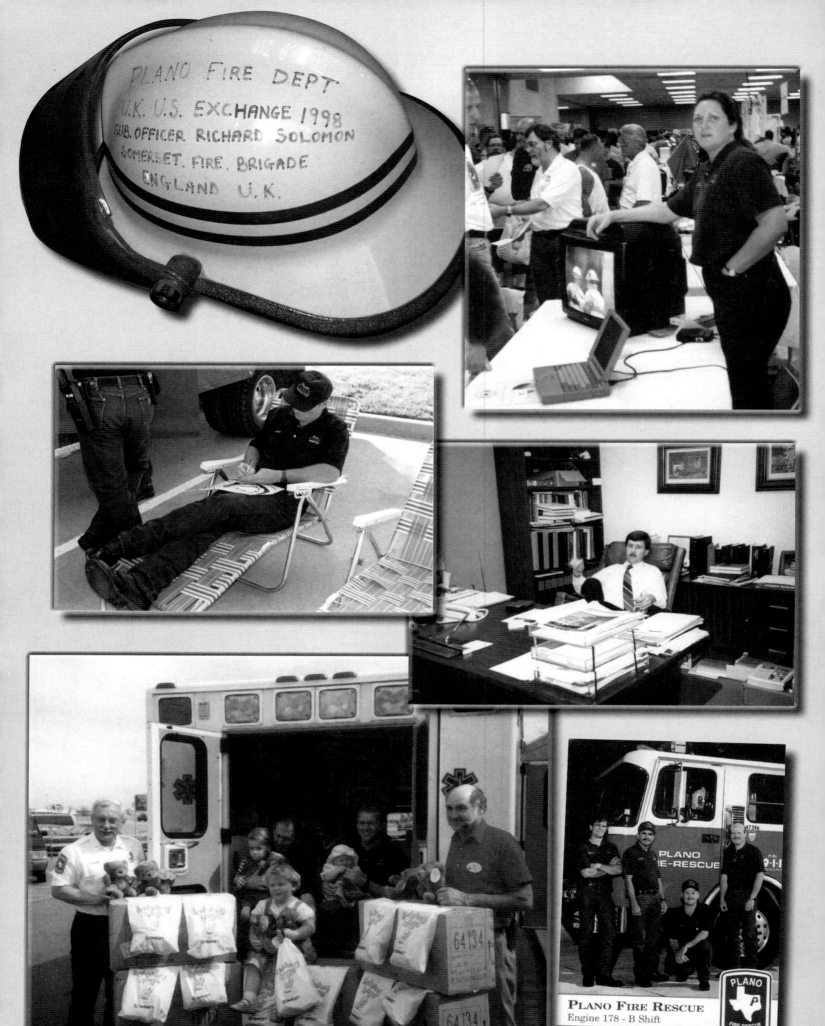

PLANO FIRE DEPT
U.K. U.S. EXCHANGE 1998
SUB. OFFICER. RICHARD SOLOMON
SOMERSET. FIRE. BRIGADE
ENGLAND U.K.

PLANO FIRE RESCUE
Engine 178 - B Shift

E8 Trading Card

125

- Plano Star Courier — Thursday, May 28, 1992

Sharon Steinman/Staff photo

Plano firefighter Ronnie Eastham of the department's swift water rescue team finishes up tying off a tow line Wednesday to a pickup that was washed into a small private lake near the corner of Preston and Parker roads by recent heavy rains. The truck was left near the lake by a Richardson resident who got stuck in the mud last week.

Missing truck turns up in rain-swollen lake

By KERI GOINS
Staff writer

What began as a joyride in the mud has ended up a very costly mistake for a Plano man.

The trouble began May 15 when the 20-year-old man de-cided to take advantage of the re-cent rains and go four-wheeling in the mud on the property of the Lakeshore on Preston housing development.

While plowing through the mud near the manmade lakes of the 377-acre development, his father's 1985 Toyota 4x4 truck that he was driving became stuck, police spokesman Sgt. Edward Brashear said.

"He went home to figure out what to do and when he came back the truck was gone. He then cal-led the Plano police to report it stolen," Brashear said.

When detectives questioned construction workers a few days later at the development, the workers said the truck was not stolen at all.

Turn to TRUCK, Page 4A

Whiffletree Fire

October 5, 1995

4:05 pm – A residential structure fire is called in to 9-1-1

4:06 pm – Engine 8 reports heavy smoke to the south and east of Station 8

4:10 pm – Frisco FD Battalion Chief notifies Plano dispatch of at least one structure and a second roof fully involved

4:10 pm – A second alarm is ordered by Engine 4

4:11 pm – A third alarm is ordered by Truck 4

4:22 pm – Command asks for an additional alarm

On a windy afternoon in October 1995, a fire started on the roof of a two-story, single family structure with a wood-shingle roof. Before seven minutes pass, all 15 Plano Fire Department units were dispatched to the scene.

Flying embers from the initial two structures ignited wood-shingles on several other homes, placing many other homes in the area at risk. When the smoke cleared and the fires were all extinguished, a total of 22 single-family homes were either damaged or destroyed.

The Whiffletree fire was fought by 93 fire personnel made up of crews from the Plano Fire Department and surrounding Richardson, Dallas, Carrollton and Frisco Fire Departments. Five patients were transported to area hospitals as a result of the fires. Two of these were Plano firefighters; one suffered heat exhaustion and one was injured by the partial collapse of a brick wall. Three citizens were transported for smoke inhalation, treated and released.

The origin of the fire is known, but the cause remains unknown.

Structure Fire Damage
Incident #95008088
October 5, 1995

Wind Direction

N

Leigh Court

T4

E4

E8

M6

R E1

E6

Leigh Drive

S2

E7

E5

T5

Wolfe Court

E2

F E1

D E13

C E114

R E3

E1

COM.

D E7

Marchman Way

Harvey Street

E3

M7

T1

Swanson Drive

C T112

Light Damage

Moderate Damage

Heavy Damage

Com.	=	Command
C	=	Carrolton
D	=	Dallas
R	=	Richardson

129

Whiffletree Fire

FIRE
1990-1999
RESCUE

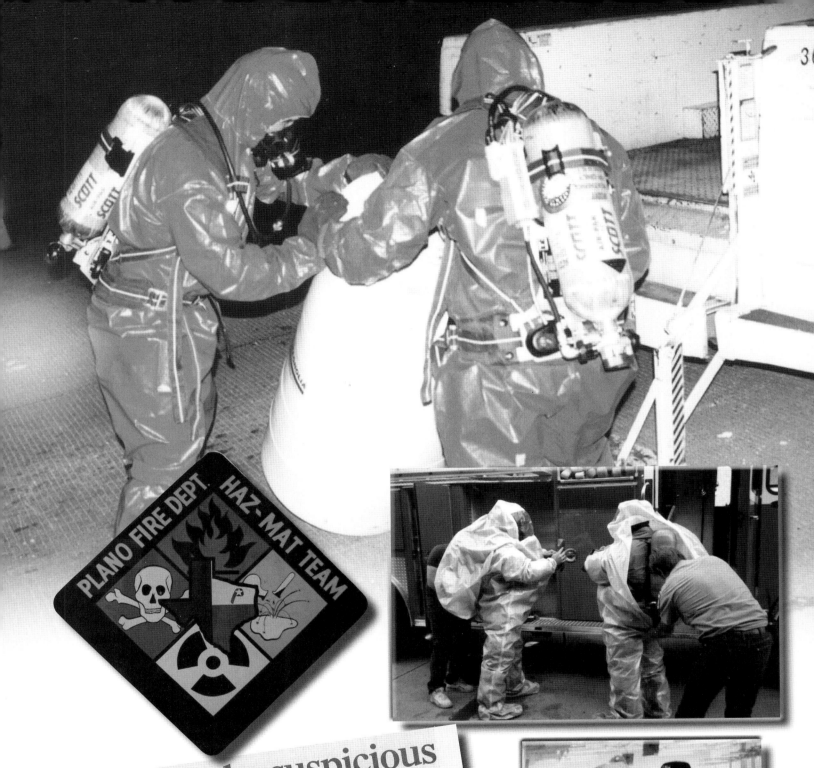

PLANO FIRE DEPT. HAZ-MAT TEAM

Hazmat checks suspicious package found in vehicle

MARTHE STINTON
mstinton@acnpapers.com

Plano police officers discovered an unknown substance Thursday afternoon while searching a vehicle in the back parking lot of the Plano Police Department.

Officers discovered an unknown powdery substance while they were searching the vehicle for narcotics.

They immediately backed off for safety and notified the Plano Fire Department's Hazardous Materials Unit for further investigation.

Plano Police Department Public Information Officer Rick McDonald said the officers took all safety precautions.

"The protocol is to back

See POLICE, Page 8A

RONNIE BAKER / STAFF PHOTO

Emergency personnel were called on to check a suspicious substance found in a vehicle parked at 909 14th St. Police are still investigating the incident.

FIRE
2000-2011
RESCUE

2000	Plano Population: 222,030
2000	Plano one of six U.S./Canadian cities selected for NFPA's *Risk Watch* implementation on elementary/middle school campuses
2000	Fire Chief Bill Peterson named *Fire Chief of the Year* by the 12,000-member International Association of Fire Chiefs
2000	Plano Fire Department is comprised of 10 fire stations, 272 civil service positions and 22 civilian positions; operates five ambulances with 151 paramedics
2001	Plano Fire Department designated an Accredited Agency with CFAI, one of only 134 agencies world-wide to attain this status
2001	343 Firefighters are killed in rescue efforts when on September 11 terrorists strike the World Trade Center in NYC, the Pentagon, and attempt to strike Washington, D. C.
2001	Plano Fire Department facilitates 770 public education programs; participates in 119 public events/festivals
2001	Community-wide "CPR Blowout" trains over 500 citizens resulting in at least one documented life-save
2001	Corporate Automatic External Defibrilator Program is initiated
2001	Plano Fire Department among first in state to use EMS training computer-programmed *Laerdal SimMan* purchased through state grant funding
2001	State-mandated five-year update to City's Emergency Disaster Plan facilitated through Fire Department.
2001	Fire Prevention Division reviewed 1,895 fire system plans for code compliance, investigated 56 fires, 33 being arson

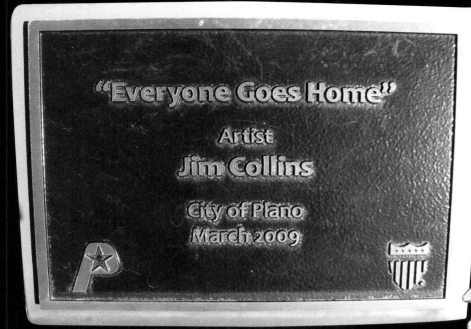

"Everyone Goes Home"

Artist
Jim Collins

City of Plano
March 2009

In March 2009 the artwork was installed in the front lawn area of Fire Administration. The piece, titled *Everyone Goes Home*, was created by Chattanooga artist Jim Collins and commissioned by the City of Plano's public art program.

Mr. Collins' inspiration for the artwork came to him during a tour of Station 1 at which he saw the words "Everyone Goes Home" on the station bay doors. The words refer to a fire service motto stating that the goal of each call to which the firefighters respond is that they and the citizens alike return home safely.

2002 • DART Electric Light Rail arrives in Plano

2002 • Plano Fire Department donates older equipment, including self-contained breathing apparatus, to Plano Sister City San Pedro Garza Garcia, Mexico

2002 • Plano Fire Explorer Post #215 garners two First Place state awards at First Annual Explorer Fire Games

2002 • Plano Fire Department received $50,000 and $273,000 Dept. of Justice grants for terrorism response equipment/education; $92,400 Fire Act FEMA Grant for emergency preparedness guide development

2002 • LAFS Clowns visited 30 elementary classrooms educating over 10,000 Plano students and teachers

2003 • 95% of customer surveys show department has *Met Expectations* or is *Better than Expected*

2003 • Citizens Fire Academy graduates 51 participants

2003 • 50-week study completed revealing current in-services ambulances are adequate and projecting future expansion planning

2003 • False Fire Alarm and Burn Permit SOP's adopted; High Rise Inspection Checklist composed and adopted

2003 • Grant-funded Residential Emergency and Disaster Initiative Handbook distributed to every Plano household by Boy and Girl Scouts

2004 • Plano Fire Department accepted into Cardiac Arrest Registry to Enhance Survival

2004 • Plano named Money Magazine #1 best place to live in the west for cities with population over 100,0000

2004 • Plano Fire Department responds to 16,220 calls for services with 5 minute 52 second fire call response time and 5 minute 35 second EMS response time

2004 • Fire Prevention Division responds to 8,180 requests for service, conducts 5,321 inspections, 875 engineering and site plan reviews, 1,437 fire protection system plan reviews

City honors firefighters for 30 years of sacrifice

By RYAN BAUER
Staff writer

One day on and two days off. That's the schedule a Plano fireman lives by, day-in and day-out. It takes a little while to get used to, firemen say, but once they do, there is no going back.

And Capts. Jimmy Bell, Jimmie O. Davidson and Dwayne Brazil haven't gone back for 30 years — since they signed on with the Plano Fire Department in 1969.

The three, who have been buddies since meeting one another on the job, recently received their 30-year recognition awards from the city in a ceremony before the City Council.

Bell, Davidson and Brazil joined the department when Plano, then population 16,000, was just a glimmer of what it is today. There was only the one fire station, which is now on the south side of the Plano Municipal Center on 15th Street and Municipal. The city's print shop and mail room now occupy the space where firemen slept, ate and parked their engines.

Back then, there were only three men to a shift and no emergency medical personnel. Each fireman had very little first-aid training, simply trying to save lives with their quick response. The same year the three became firemen, a state law was passed, requiring fire departments to provide that emergency care. Prior to that, funeral homes had the monopoly on ambulances.

Bell, who has been off-shift for some years, started his career in February 1969, at the age of 28, hoping to follow in his father's footsteps. He remembers being 8 years old and going out with his twin brother to fires that their volunteer fireman father worked on.

"It's a dangerous job at times," said Bell. "Things are going to

Turn to SERVICE, Page 4A

Service

From 1A

happen. There's a lot of times you're here and you want to be with your family — like after a tornado or something like that because you don't know whether they're hurt or not."

He and the other two vividly remember a pair of fires that ravaged the downtown area in the early '70s.

"They were just about more than we could handle," Bell said. "We had lots of help come in."

Davidson said those blazes put every firefighter to the test.

"Sometimes you see something like that you're up against, and it just overwhelms you," he said. "You think, 'What am I doing here?' But, you just shake it off, get your second wind, go on about your business and do what you can do."

All three agreed the biggest changes between 1969 and 2000 have to do with improved equipment and better training. But Bell said it seems like there are less fires today than when he started.

"The biggest thing is so many wrecks," he said. "We've got wrecks all day long. From the time people start work 'til after they get home at night, and then we still have a few stragglers. If people ever start driving right, they'd probably be laying (firefighters) off around here."

Ryan Bauer/Staff photo
Plano firemen, from left, Dwayne Brazil, Jimmie O. Davidson and Jimmy Bell, recently were recognized for 30 years of service with the City of Plano.

Saying
Good-by

The City o
Plano's sen
employee,
Capt. Jimm
(left), calle
quits last m
after 33 yea
Although
became a
firefighter
1969, he ac
began his
vice in 196
volunteer.

...ell (top) wished his broth-...fishing with a new rod...d from the family. Above, ...gratulates Capt. Jimmy...n who moved up as the ...st senior employee with ...'s retirement.

Friends from "the old days" — former assistant chief Paul Mayfield (above) and his wife, Pat, made the trek from their retirement home at Lake Texoma to share a another laugh with Bell, a notorious jokester.

Plano City Councilman Ken Lambert (left) was on hand to offer the city's compliments and recall his days thirty years ago as city manager of

Division Chief George Cardwell (abo... helps Bell settle into his new retiremen... rocker complete with a personalized b... for his lap.

FIRE
2000-2011
RESCUE

ausey   Rick Thomas   Roger Smith   Dwayne Brazil   John Housewright   John Lewis   Vic Cowdrey   George Caldwell

Plano's first professional firefighters retire

Group of 8 started at less than $2 an hour

BY PAUL MEYER
STAFF WRITER

Hired more than three decades ago to serve a city of 1,800 residents, eight of Plano's first batch of full-time fighters are retiring from service – leaving behind a than 240 years of accumulated experi-

George Cald

FIRE CHIEF

"There was so much change in the department over my 30 years, it is difficult to imagine, and I consider myself fortunate to have been there. I got to work with, and learn from, so many good and dedicated people. Being a member of the Plano Fire Department was both the greatest opportunity and experience of my life. Other than my family, it is the thing of which I am most proud."

~ *Kirk Owen, Assistant Chief, Retired*

FIRE RESCUE
2000-2011

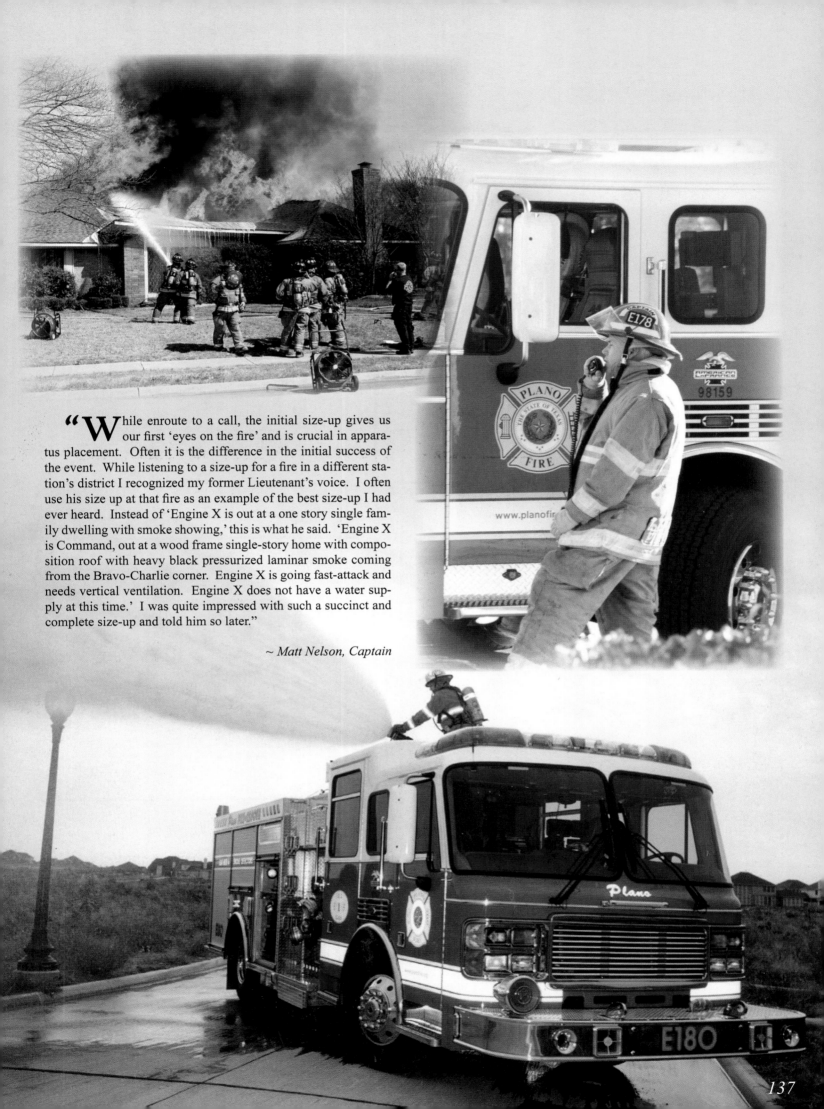

"While enroute to a call, the initial size-up gives us our first 'eyes on the fire' and is crucial in apparatus placement. Often it is the difference in the initial success of the event. While listening to a size-up for a fire in a different station's district I recognized my former Lieutenant's voice. I often use his size up at that fire as an example of the best size-up I had ever heard. Instead of 'Engine X is out at a one story single family dwelling with smoke showing,' this is what he said. 'Engine X is Command, out at a wood frame single-story home with composition roof with heavy black pressurized laminar smoke coming from the Bravo-Charlie corner. Engine X is going fast-attack and needs vertical ventilation. Engine X does not have a water supply at this time.' I was quite impressed with such a succinct and complete size-up and told him so later."

~ Matt Nelson, Captain

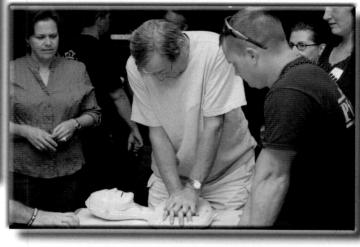

'Second Birthday' celebrates a life saved

BY JOSH HIXSON
STAFF WRITER

A second chance at life is an event worth celebrating, according to Dani Dooley.

Members of the Plano Fire Department, Dani and his family celebrated his "Second Birthday" Tuesday afternoon at the fire administration building.

Dani, a 35-year-old husband and father of two, was playing hockey with friends at the Dr Pepper Star Center in Plano on May 13 when the unthinkable occurred that evening.

After the game, Dani said he had some trouble breathing and felt a pain in his chest. Symptoms his wife Karen quickly chalked up to a cold.

As Dani headed toward the parking lot, things began to take a turn for the worse.

"I was walking out into the parking lot and, to be honest with you, that is all I remember," Dani said. "I made it out to the parking lot and collapsed right there at the car. The next thing I remember when I woke up I was in the hospital."

Paramedics and fire rescue specialists David Schott and Art Lujan arrived on the scene about 11:30 p.m. and found Dani near death.

"In all real terms he had passed away. His heart was basically just quivering in his chest," Schott said. "It was not producing any sort of pulse. He was not circulating any blood, not getting any oxygen to any of his cells."

Schott said they would later learn Dani had a 100 percent occluded left anterior descending artery.

A blockage in this artery is so grave it is termed a "widow maker." Most people who experience this type of heart attack do not survive Dani was told.

It took three electrical shocks from a defibrillator before Dani's heart started responding, Schott said.

Once he arrived at the hospital Dani was taken to a catheterization laboratory where his blockage was removed and replaced with a stint. After doctors performed an angioplasty Dani remained in a coma for five days, Karen said.

"For 48 hours I sat there and tried to think of how I was going to bury my husband," Karen said. "I am so thankful that I didn't have to do that."

Nearly 10 months later Dani celebrated his survival by being presented with an automated external defibrillator (AED) from paramedics Schott and Lujan that was donated by the Zoll Medical Corporation.

An AED is used to shock the heart back into a normal rhythm with an electric current during sudden cardiac arrest.

The Dooleys said having the AED will give them some peace of mind now that they have moved out to Weatherford where they said the emergency medical response time was not as quick.

"The defibrillator will give me a peace of mind and some relief that at least if (sudden) cardiac arrest) happens we will be prepared," Karen said.

Officials at the ceremony praised the quick response time and life saving efforts of the emergency medical services team which they said were instrumental in saving Dani's life.

See BIRTHDAY, Page 4A

David Schott, a paramedic and fire rescue specialist with the Plano Fire Department, presents Dani Dooley and his wife Karen with an automated external defibrillator donated by the Zoll Medical Corporation Tuesday afternoon. Dooley suffered from sudden cardiac arrest after playing a game of hockey at the Dr Pepper Star Center in Plano on May 13. To purchase this photo and others visit MyCapture at scntx.com.

JAMIE MITCHELL/STAFF PHOTO

FIRST A

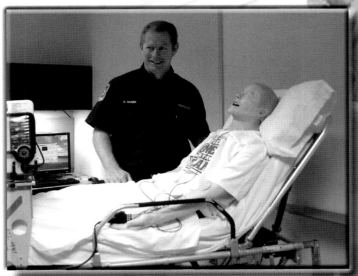

"Thanks to dedicated personnel and a rigorous EMS training program, the Plano Fire Department (PFD) consistently provides the highest level of care to patients experiencing emergencies. Through training and partnership with local hospitals the PFD consistently provides some of the fastest heart attack treatment times ever documented.

The care of our most critically ill patient - the patient in cardiac arrest - has evolved into a finely tuned care sequence. The PFD has undertaken extensive training on the "pit crew" concept of CPR and on the importance of continuous compressions. Plano was among the first to adopt the Autopulse and the EZ IO. The Autopulse provides reliable, effective compressions allowing PFD personnel to focus on other aspects of resuscitation. The EZ IO provides rapid intraosseous access for fluid and medication administration. Combined, these two devices have simplified and improved our care and our cardiac arrest survival rate. The PFD also uses web-based transmission of 12 lead ECGs from the point of contact with a patient to diagnose heart attack and expedite treatment at the receiving hospital.

In 2010, Plano became the first EMS system in north Texas to employ therapeutic hypothermia for the medical cardiac arrest patient. This treatment involves PFD personnel lowering the patient's core temperature through ice packs and chilled IV fluids. The therapy proves a neuroprotective effect which has resulted in improved neurologic outcomes among cardiac arrest survivors.

The PFD participates in ongoing medical research on many levels. This includes the CDC/Emory/AHA supported CARES Database (Cardiac Arrest Registry to Enhance Survival) and the ROC (Resuscitations Outcomes Consortium). The ROC is a group of metropolitan areas across the United States and Canada that will perform multiple ongoing pre-hospital emergency medicine studies funded by the National Institutes of Health.

Finally, the PFD has embarked on an innovative training program. Interactive continuing education combined with a cadaver lab program, paramedic shadowing of emergency physicians, and simulation training with a high fidelity wireless mannequin help PFD personnel stay at a constant state of readiness for the emergency patient."

~ Dr. Mark Gamber,
PFD Medical Director

Plano Fire Department to hold exam for firefighter eligibility list

ZACH MARKOVIC
zmarkovic@acnpapers.com

Even with constraints from city budget issues, public safety remains a top priority for the Plano Fire Department.

In an effort to create a pool from which to choose potential firefighter candidates in case a vacancy should arise, the fire department will hold an entrance examination for the fire rescue specialist position at 6 p.m. Sept.

27 at the Plano Centre. The cutoff date to apply for the exam is Sept. 2.

Those who take the written exam begin the process needed to become a Plano firefighter. Their score will place them on a list of possible candidates to continue on with their application.

"The exam makes you eligible for the next step," said Capt. Floyd Jones, fire department spokesman. "Each step presents potential pitfalls and you have to navigate them better than the

competition."

There have been changes to the system with which potential applicants had to comply in order to be eligible. Previously, applicants were required to hold both a firefighter certification from the Texas Commission on Fire Protection and an emergency medical technician certification from the Texas Department of State Health Services. In addition, applicants were required to have a high school diploma and completed 30 college hours to be eligible to take the entrance examination.

Jones said in an effort to level the playing field for those who might not be able to afford going through certification course, changes were approved by the Civil Service Commission to allow applicants to have only a high school diploma and 30 college hours to be eligible to take the

See FIRE, Page 2A

DAN BURKE / PFRA MEMBER

Fire rescue specialist Michael Lewis, fire apparatus operator Kelly Kuropata and fire apparatus operator Aaron Deary work as a team to help put out a fire last year. The Plano Fire Department will hold an exam on Sept. 27 for future firefighter applicants. The cutoff day for signing up for the exam is Thursday.

Serving as Plano's Fire Chief since 1982, William E. Peterson retired in 2006. Under his leadership the department became the first in the nation to achieve both Fire and Emergency Medical Service Accreditation, today remaining the largest Insurance Services Office Class 1 city in the nation carrying both Accreditations. The department became one of the first in Texas to require all personnel be fully cross-trained in fire fighting and emergency medical services and under his tenure Fire Stations 5 through 11 were placed on the grid. Peterson helped make the Plano Fire Department nationally and internationally known for its focus on customer service, public fire and life safety education, training and Homeland Security readiness. In his alternate role as Plano's Emergency Management Director he led the City's 2005 assistance efforts in sheltering over 500 Gulf Coast evacuees from back-to-back Hurricanes Katrina and Rita. His accolades included 2000 *Fire Chief of the Year* from the 12,000+ member International Association of Fire Chiefs and being named *International President of the Institution of Fire Engineers* in 2004. Named in his honor, in October 2010 the 16,434 square foot William E. Peterson Emergency Operations Center opened serving as the City's training facility and the command, control and coordination point for the City's emergency operations.

FIRE
2000-2011
RESCUE

This flag, flown over the United States Capitol, is given to the dedicated individuals of the Plano Fire Department by U.S. Congressman Sam Johnson on the 11th day of September, 2009. This flag is given in honor of their service to our community.

Sam Johnson, Member of Congress
3rd District of Texas

September 11, 2009

U.S. HOUSE OF REPRESENTATIVES

"Although chaplains have provided support to our firefighters since the early 1900's it wasn't until 1989 that the official chaplaincy for the department was established. Our first responsibility is to the men and women of the fire service and their families. In turn, we join them in serving the citizens of Plano with comfort and support in the initial stage of grief over the loss of loved ones. Support for those tough calls in the form of critical incident stress debriefing for the firefighters is also provided. Formal occasions such as memorial services, promotions, retirements and station openings are usually attended by prayer by one of the chaplains. It is always a privilege when we are called upon to serve alongside those who serve."

*Robert Matthews,
Senior Chaplain*

Plano
All-America City

"We still stand united and we always will."

That's the message being echoed all along the travel route of the now famous Patriot Flag. This iconic symbol of American heroics made a momentous stop in Plano on April 9th, 2011. Flown from a Plano Fire Department aerial ladder truck at Haggard Park, the Patriot Flag toured "50 States in 50 Weeks" as a tribute to members of the armed forces, first responders, those fallen Americans of the 9/11 attacks and their families.

"When a firefighter was killed in the line of duty, the Irish ensured their fallen brothers were buried with full honors, making the bagpipe the adoptive instrument of the fire department. Today, that time-honored music crosses all ethnic, racial and religious lines and is played at funerals regardless of race, color or creed. We have been called upon to lead graduating college students, welcome newly built stations, and announce the arrival of new firefighters into this proud profession. While many of these occasions have been grand celebrations, sadly many were to help family and friends in our profession in dire need. In that respect, the crown of loyalty has come to signify the commitment that we have towards each other and the public in general. Our mission is to help foster the Irish heritage and traditions within the fire service and to promote and preserve the accomplishments firefighters have made and continue to make every day. We will continue to support and improve the community through good works, and to constantly look for new ways to make a positive impact upon the communities we proudly serve."

~ Craig Swaner, Fire Rescue Specialist
and Plano P&D Band Member

146

" **A**s one of the original seven members of the Plano Fire Department Honor Guard there were many proud moments but these most stand out in my mind. A few weeks after 9-11 we attended the Fallen Firefighters Memorial in Emmitsburg, Maryland where President Bush spoke of the fallen's heroism. Afterwards we drove to Ground Zero and were able to meet with some of the FDNY guys attending the funeral of one their fallen, Andrew Fredricks of Squad 18, the following day. It was a humbling experience. On the first anniversary of 9-11 we made a return trip to Ground Zero as part of the largest gathering of firefighters in history, many from around the world. It was an amazing show of uniforms and esprit de corps as we marched together up Broadway to Madison Square Garden for the memorial."

~ Steve Reynolds,
Fire Rescue Specialist

FIRE
2000-2011
RESCUE

Oct. 2006	Plano stations are designated *Safe Baby Sites* by Baby Moses organization for no-question infant protection drop-off
Aug. 2004	Plano Fire Department participates in FEMA-funded Integrated Emergency Management Course at National Fire Academy, Emmitsburg, Maryland
2006	Plano Fire Rescue *File of Life* packets made available to the public
Jul. 2005	*Battle of the Badges* blood drive initiated between Fire/Police/Carter BloodCare
2006	EMS Section Adopted the American Heart Association 2005 guidelines for Cardiopulmonary Resuscitation and Emergency Cardiovascular Care
Jan. 2005	Office of Homeland Security is created operating under direction of Fire Chief/Emergency Management Director, Bill Peterson
2006	*AutoPulse* mechanical CPR device and *EZ-IO* device for delivery of drugs and fluids introduced to improve cardiac arrest survival rates
2005	Urban Search and Rescue vehicle purchased with $250,000 in Federal grant funds
2006	Stand-alone Department of Homeland Security formed separated from Fire
2006	Plano receives *Safe Community* designation from *National Fire Protection Association* for education efforts
2006	PFRA and PFFA restore 1982 American La France fire engine
2006	Six *Community Emergency Response Training* classes graduate 108.
2006	Station No. 11 opens, 4800 Los Rios Blvd.
2006	Mobile Command Post vehicle purchased for approximately $650,000

Plano Star Courier sunday

STARLOCALNEWS.COM

VOLUME 122, NO. 4

OCTOBER 24, 2010

Safe city gets a little Safer

The city of Plano opened the doors to the completed facility of Fire Station No. 12 on Friday morning.

ZACH MARKOVIC / STAFF PHOTO

Fire Station No. 12 adds to emergency services

ZACH MARKOVIC
zmarkovic@acnpapers.com

Not resting upon its laurels as the nation's safest city, Plano is preparing to emergency facility aimed at focusing disaster relief efforts.

Fire Station 12, Fire Logistics Warehouse and the William E. Peterson Emer- though quite the mouthful to say, is a three-in-one center combining efforts from the fire department and emergency services in Plano.

The facility was dedi- 10:30 a.m. Oct. 22 at 4101 West Parker Road.

The Fire Station and Logistics Warehouse has been in operation since December 2009, with the dedication

---

2006 • Fire Chief William E. Peterson retires; Assistant Chief Bob Acker serves as interim Fire Chief

2007 • Plano Fire Department responds to 18,964 calls for service with 11,734 requiring EMS response; response from dispatch to arrival 5 minutes 10 seconds; response from receipt in dispatch to arrival 5 minutes 48 seconds

2007 • New mobile command post placed into service

2007 • Two Heritage Grants from Fireman's Fund received: $45,000 for public education materials; $5,781 for conversion from VHS to DVD education materials

2007 • Fire Prevention Division responds to 11,028 service requests including 6,860 systems inspections, 759 engineering reviews, 1,873 fire system plan reviews

2007 • Dr. Mark Gamber appointed Medical Director

FIRE RESCUE
2000-2011

Emergency management director touts station's location

CONTINUED FROM 1A

awaiting the completion of the emergency operations

ambulance, battalion chief and the department's utility (light and air) vehicle, according to a city release.

for all firefighting and emergency medical services equipment, supply, uniforms, personal protective

the city's emergency operations during large emergencies, disasters and major events, City county

gives us a lot more agencies on the table."

The U.S. Green Building

tioning systems. More than 40 percent of the construction materials were locally

Various local dignitaries and government officials past and present visited the dedication of Fire Station 12 and the various centers attached to the facility.

152

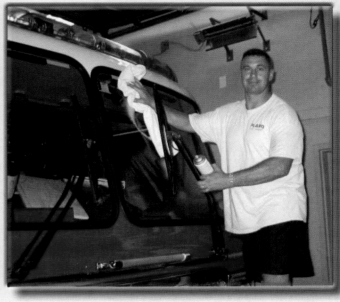

"When I am at work I miss my family very much…more than anything. But I love this great profession immensely and look forward to my time at the firehouse with the crew. In a 30 year career, a fireman will spend 10 years at the firehouse. That is a lot of time away from those you love. As you can see by the smile on my son Chandler's face, he too loves being at the firehouse. He constantly asks to go to the station and see the pumpers, trucks and "the Guys." Young or old, it seems you can never get away from the magic that the "Big Red Trucks" bring into our lives and imaginations."

~ *Captain Scott Mallen, 6C*

2007 ● Seventh full-time ambulance added to fleet

2007 ● Special Operations Battalion Chief added to coordinate Haz Mat, Search & Rescue and Swiftwater Rescue

2007 ● Hugo R. Esparza, Fort Worth Fire Department Assistant Chief, named Plano Fire Chief

"Let no man's ghost
    return to say his
training let him down."

~ *Firefighters Saying*

156

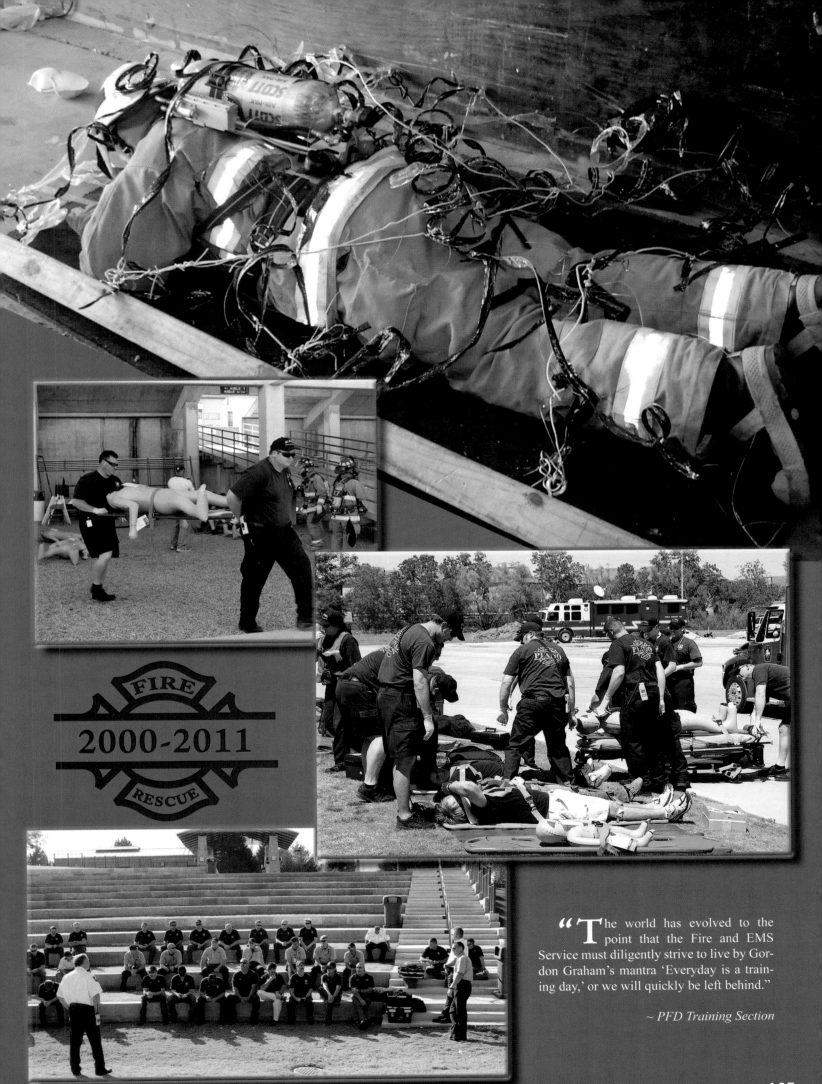

FIRE

2000-2011

RESCUE

"The world has evolved to the point that the Fire and EMS Service must diligently strive to live by Gordon Graham's mantra 'Everyday is a training day,' or we will quickly be left behind."

~ *PFD Training Section*

PLANO STAR COURIER ★ THURSDAY, DECEMBER 23, 2010

StarLocalNews.com

Residents get hands on with fire department

ZACH MARKOVIC
zmarkovic@acnpapers.com

The closest most residents come to the Plano Fire Department is on the streets as a fire truck or ambulance rushes past them on their way to an emergency.

In an effort to give residents a glimpse of the everyday workings of the fire department — and a greater insight into what their taxes mean for its operations — the Citizens Fire Academy was created.

Applications for the first of two courses next year are currently being accepted. Since the class is capped at 30 students, space is limited for each session and usually fills up quickly, said Plano Fire Department spokeswoman Peggy Harrell.

The Citizens Fire Academy is a lecture and hands-on experience that gives adults the opportunity to learn more about what their fire department is about. According to the fire department's website, the academy is open to persons 18 and older who either live or work in the city of Plano and is free of charge. The class meets one night a week at the Fire Administration building on Avenue K.

Each night, CFA participants learn about a differ-

the stereotype of the firefighter so people know that we are not 'just a bunch of guys sitting around and waiting for fire,' like some people say," Harrell said.

She said firefighters go beyond just fighting fires. They regularly perform community education and outreach so residents can practice more safety in their lives.

used with the work, Harrell said. After a lecture, the class goes out and tours whatever was just discussed.

Beyond staying near the classroom, students will go through the firefighting tactics that range from dealing with night fires in a residential home to office fires in the day. All of this leads up to the day when

2009	Station No. 12 opens (4101 W. Parker Rd.) in complex with new Fire Logistics Warehouse and William E. Peterson Emergency Operations Center
2010	Plano Fire Department initiates Hands-Only CPR training for all City of Plano employees
2011	Plano Population: 261,350
2011	Fire Station No. 13 opens, 6901 Corporate Drive

FIRE
2000-2011
RESCUE

"First and foremost, I see the CFA as an opportunity to educate our community. A large portion of our citizens see us, but do not really know us. This is an opportunity for us to display and explain what it is that we do. In some cases, it will be the only opportunity to interface with our citizens to this extent."

--*Hugo R. Esparza, Fire Chief*

VOLUME 118, NO. 140

In the Community. With the Community. For the Community.

SUNDAY, APRIL 29, 2007

Fired-up friends:

The tale of 3 ladies' adventure with the Plano Citizens Fire Academy

JOSH HIXSON
STAFF WRITER

Three friends are on a mission.

A mission to learn as much about Plano's city services as they can and have an adventure to remember in the process.

The Citizens Fire Academy has provided the type of education and excitement Debbie Cason, Mary Beth Motney and Tammy Browning said they were looking for.

"The first call that I had I was real excited when the alarm went off," Motney said, as she described her first ride-a-long with the fire department. "They said it was time to go, and I got in the truck. Then I started getting real scared. I thought 'Oh my gosh.' I wanted to go, but I didn't want it to be bad for anyone."

The academy is a 10-week class that meets once a week at the fire administration building on Avenue K. Each class is designed to teach participants about a different topic concerning the fire department. They also get to try on fire-fighting equipment, drive a fire truck and ride out on a fire truck when fire fighters respond to an emergency call.

See CFA, Page 3A

SUBMITTED PHOTO
Debbie Cason (left), Mary Beth Motney (center) and Tammy Browning joined the Plano Citizens Fire Academy and found fun and education in the 10-week class.

VOLUME 121, NO. 192

NIGHT OUT in
the neighborhood

AY, OCT 5, 2010

'We have one of the lowest
crime rates for a city
our size in the nation'

ZACH MARKOVIC

One of the easiest steps
to prevent crime is simply
taking a step out the front
door and shaking your
neighbor's hand.

Getting to know neighbors and the surrounding
community around residents is one of the main
goals of National Night Out
which over 65 communities
in Plano participated in
Wednesday night. The
event encouraged residents
to organize block-style picnics in order provide a
chance for neighbors to
meet each other.

is important that you all
know each other, know the
good guys from the bad
guys and know your neighbors from the strangers. It
makes our city better.

And Plano has proof of
its citizen crime watch program is making it better.
Plano Police Department
Chief Gregory Rushin said
the proof was in the recent
award received from the
National Sheriff's Association for an exemplary crime
watch program in the nation.

"That is because of the
citizens we have here,"
Rushin said. "We have one

"**B**efore the PFD adopted Sparky the Fire Dog as our official mascot, there was Fire Cat. He was a cat who fought fire…I think. I heard once that he was a cat to honor the Plano Senior High Schools' mascots, a wildcat and a panther. Anyway, I'm glad that we've adopted Sparky. We've had a couple of great volunteers as Sparky. PFRA member Rob Johnson is the best. But, every year Battalion Chief Harrell has helped as Sparky and I rang the Salvation Army kettle bell. It's hard for people to walk by Sparky and not put a little money in the kettle."

*~ Captain Peggy Harrell,
Fire Safety Education Coordinator*

DOING
THE MOST
GOOD

FIRE
2000-2011
RESCUE

"Education is the most effective weapon in the Plano Fire Department's arsenal of fire and injury prevention tools, with all the Fire Department personnel as active participants in the educational efforts."

- Captain Peggy Harrell,
Fire Safety Education Coordinator

No clowning arou

JAMIE MITCHELL/STAFF PHOTO

Plano Fire Department's Snozzle the Clown, top left, Patches and sheriff Sam (far right) introduces Meg Blasingame to their puppet assistants following their afternoon show at Stinson Elementry School. Snozzle, played by Chris Jefferson of Station #1, Patches, played by Calvin Cook of Station #7 and Sheriff Sam, played by David Edwards of Station #8 make the rounds to the local elementry schools teaching children "safety rules" for everyday living. The team's entertaining ways include skits, puppets and sing-a-long songs with the children.

SAFETY RULES

PFD educates public on fire and life safety

JOSH HIXSON
STAFF WRITER

Mrs. O'Leary's cows may have been responsible for the one of the largest and most infamous fires in U.S. history.

At least the notorious cows are what some claim instigated the Great Chicago Fire that killed more than 250 people, burned 2,000 acres of property and destroyed more than 17,400 structures.

According to the popular and widely disputed version of the

story on Oct. 8, 1871, one of Mrs. O'Leary's five cows kicked over a lamp. The lamp then set the barn on fire and eventually spread throughout the entire city. The blaze was still going strong well into the next day.

Some historians, who deny the validity of "the cow theory," have offered other causes such as thrown cigarettes or meteorites that happened to fall that day. Regardless of the legitimacy of these causes, the Chicago Fire _____ — the _____ red the

same day, served to leave a lasting reminder of the devastation that fires can cause.

Forty-nine years later President Woodrow Wilson made the first National Fire Prevention Day Proclamation.

Fire Prevention Week is now a nationally observed public safety week aimed at growing public awareness about fire prevention methods. National Fire Prevention Week is observed on the Sunday through Saturday period in which Oct. 9 occurs.

See FIRE, Page 4A

FIRE
2000-2011
RESCUE

FIRE

2000-2011

RESCUE

It looked like the end of the road for Engine 189. Activated in 1982 and retired from reserve service in 1997, the 1982 American LaFrance engine sat in open storage at the City's fleet services lot, a rusting by-product of Plano's growth and new technology. Rusted metal, shattered equipment gauges, broken windows and faded paint signaled the end to the engine that provided public safety services during the height of an explosion of growth and prosperity. As new equipment and engines were incorporated into service, Engine 189 had slowly climbed down the ladder of usefulness. Now it sat abandoned with only its motor maintained and ready for action. As the new millennium dawned so did the effort to resuscitate Engine 189. The Plano Fire Rescue Associates (PFRA) looked beyond the effects of Mother Nature and envisioned an opportunity for a vehicle that could be used in parades, for education and for the solemn duty of ceremonial burial transport. Following PFRA fundraisers, donations from individuals and businesses, it was Local 2149, the International Association of Firefighters, who ultimately provided the remaining needed funds that secured the restoration. After six months of hands-on work, the project was completed and the newly restored engine was unveiled at a ceremony at Station 1, January 29, 2005. The engine is now housed at Station 7, a proud reminder that equipment, as well as man, has protected the community through service in the Plano Fire Department.

"As I recall, PFRA member Jeff Allbritten and PFD Division Chief Kirk Owen had talked about doing this restoration for several years but it never got past the "talking phase". In 2003 PFRA members voted to take action and make the restoration a reality. We formed a Restoration Committee. The first meeting was in my kitchen! We had fun. I have been most gratified that the Honor Guard has now claimed the engine as its own and holds it in the high regard it deserves. I think the restored ALF serves the Fire Department and the PFD firefighters well."

--Marcia Hurst,
PFRA Member and Member of 1982
American La France Restoration Committee

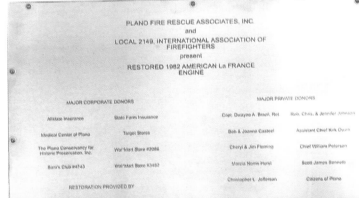

PLANO COURIER

Star

Inside
Students remember 9/11
Yavneh Academy students commemorate those who died in terror attacks.
— See Page 2A

Sports
West knocks off East
No. 3 state-ranked Lady Wolves defeat No. 20 Lady Panthers in four games.
— See Page 1B

136

WEDNESDAY, SEPTEMBER 13, 2006

Esparza named fire chief

New head of Fire and Rescue seeks to build upon successes

JOSHUA C. JOHNSON
STAFF WRITER

When it comes to emergency services, Hugo R. Esparza is con-... he had the training, education and experience for his new position as Plano's new fire chief.

"It's a very unique opportunity I'm thrilled and both humbled and privileged," said Esparza. This is a plum job. This is a great department, great city. I feel real fortunate to be given the opportunity."

A native of Fort Worth, Esparza brings a wealth of experience from the Forth Worth fire department where he has served for the last 32 years.

He has moved through the department as Engineer/Fire Suppression, Lieutenant/Fire Suppression, Captain/Fire Suppression, Captain/Human Resources Officer, Executive Deputy Fire Chief/Human Resources Division, Deputy Fire Chief/Operations Division, and his current position as Executive Deputy Fire Chief, Executive Services Division.

Because of his achievements, Esparza will officially take office in Plano around mid-November. He and his wife will soon relocate from Fort Worth to Plano in the upcoming months.

"One of the things that I was looking at is that I wanted to try and find a department in the area," he said. "Because both me and my wife were born and raised in Fort Worth."

See NEW, Page 3A

Hugo R. Esparza

Hugo Esparza became Plano's 18th Fire Chief on November 27, 2006, having previously served 31 years with the Fort Worth Fire Department where he was Deputy Chief of the Executive Services Division. "He has risen through the ranks of fire service in Fort Worth and brings to Plano his wide base of knowledge," said then Plano City Manager Tom Muehlenbeck in announcing his appointment. "His experience in responding to large scale disasters will be invaluable to our community and he is a progressive and proven leader."

Chief Esparza has an extensive background in the fire service, which began in January 1975, and includes fire-fighting, EMS, HazMat, technical rescue, bomb squad unit, training officer, fire prevention, fire investigations, public fire education, recruiting, and human resources administration. He holds a Master of Liberal Arts from Texas Christian University and a Bachelor of Science in Emergency Administration and Planning – Cum Laude – from the University of North Texas. In addition, he is a graduate of the Executive Fire Officer Program through the National Fire Academy and is a fellow of the Senior Executives in State and Local Government Program through the Kennedy School of Government at Harvard University.

With 24 years spent in the field providing fire and rescue services, 17 on the truck, he stated, "I always try to keep in mind that I don't forget where I came from and what the firefighters are experiencing on the fire trucks. Firefighting is constantly changing so experiences are always changing. Anything that I do we will get done together and come to that decision together."

FIRE
2000-2011
RESCUE

Founded in 1972 by members of the Plano Fire Department, IAFF Local 2149 has worked closely over the years with Fire administration and elected officials to advance safe working conditions, fair wages and secure well-funded retirement. The Local has also initiated and/or supported fire station expansion, fire apparatus, medic units, and maintaining an ISO Class 1 rating, a reflection of delivery of the highest levels of community fire service. Voluntary payment of monthly dues ensures resources on hand for promotion and resolution of common issues and provision of a benevolence fund that routinely cares for brothers and sisters in need. Major milestones of Local 2149 include the adoption of State Civil Service rules, increased employee retirement contributions and Fair Labor and Standards Acts overtime pay calculations, a minimum of four firefighters staffing apparatus 24/7, workers compensation case representation and State legislation addressing firefighter heart attacks. In 2010 the Local purchased a stand-alone office/meeting hall adjacent the City's Municipal Center complex on Municipal Drive. 2011 saw the Local honored with a stairwell support beam World Trade Center artifact for eventual public display, presented by the City of New York Port Authority.

PLANO FIREFIGHTERS ASSOCIATION

LOCAL 2149

EST. 1972

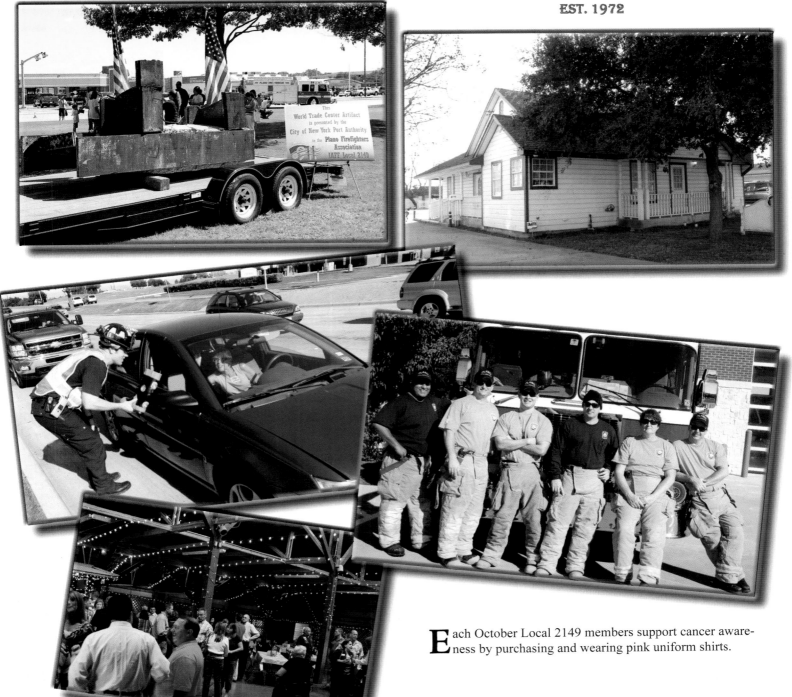

Each October Local 2149 members support cancer awareness by purchasing and wearing pink uniform shirts.

When the September 23, 2005, call went out for assistance to transport Hurricane Rita coastal evacuee patients to local hospitals, two Plano Fire Rescue med units took their place in a line of Metroplex medical teams lined up along a Love Field runway. Armed with ear plugs and little direction, their professionalism and compassion soon provided a calming environment for the persons in their charge. "We were given two patients to transport to a Los Colinas hospital who had been airlifted from a South Texas hospital. We were not provided medical information on the patients, one of whom did not speak English and the other who required constant medical attention. Everything, however, ran smoothly. I was very impressed with the training I had been given by the City of Plano and felt like I had a very good idea of how the system worked and what was expected of me. When we pulled up to the incident, it ran very close to our practice runs in Plano."

*- Patricia Swavey,
Fire Rescue Specialist*

VOLUME 121, NO. 142   In the Community. With the Community. For the Community.   FRIDAY, JUNE 25, 2010

Boys rescued from rushing water

JON VANDERLAAN
jvanderlaan@scnpapers.com

Afternoon rain resulted in an emergency call at 3:13 p.m. Thursday under Parker Road at White Rock Creek as three boys were found stranded underneath the bridge.

All three were successfully rescued and were not hurt, said Forest Harrell, Plano Fire Department battalion chief.

The three boys, two 13-year-olds and a 14-year-old, were on a small fishing boat floating down the creek when the current and water level picked up because of rain earlier in the afternoon, he said.

The boys launched the boat from a house up the river, and lost control of it when waters picked up, Harrell said. They found a safe place under the bridge standing on a concrete support.

The first responders on the scene made initial contact with the boys, told them to stay where they were and prepared in case one of them fell in the water, he said.

Although the water was only up to their ankles when they stood on the support, Harrell said the water level was about four feet higher than normal and the boys would have been

taken away by the current if they fell from the support.

The PFD swift water team was the next to respond, and threw life vests to the boys and told them to tie themselves to the support with a provided rope, he said.

The team then used a motorized, inflatable raft to travel upstream to rescue the three boys.

Harrell said because Plano is well known for flash flooding, people should stay away from rivers or creeks after a rain.

"It's a terrible thing to do around Plano," he said. "Water comes up really fast around here. It dissipates quick, but it comes up quick."

Harrell also said debris that rushes downstream could endanger a person in the river after rain.

The force of the water could even move a car if the water is high enough, despite the slow speed of the water, he said.

ZACH MARKOVIC / STAFF PHOTO
Three boys were rescued Thursday from under Parker Road at White Rock Creek after rains caused them to lose control of a small boat they were operating. Plano Fire Department crews responded after receiving the call at 3:13 p.m. Thursday.

"The Plano Fire Department supports the Plano community through many civic activities such as the Carter Blood Bank's annual Battle of the Badges blood drive, a friendly competition between our Plano Fire and Plano Police teams. Participants throughout the community who donate blood may cast their vote for one of the two competing "badges." Although the trophy has been somewhat elusive, the real winners are the people who receive much needed blood through this competition."

~ Hugo Esparza, Fire Chief

FIRE
2000-2011
RESCUE

BLOOD DRIVE

BATTLE OF THE BADGES

VOTE FOR FIRE !!

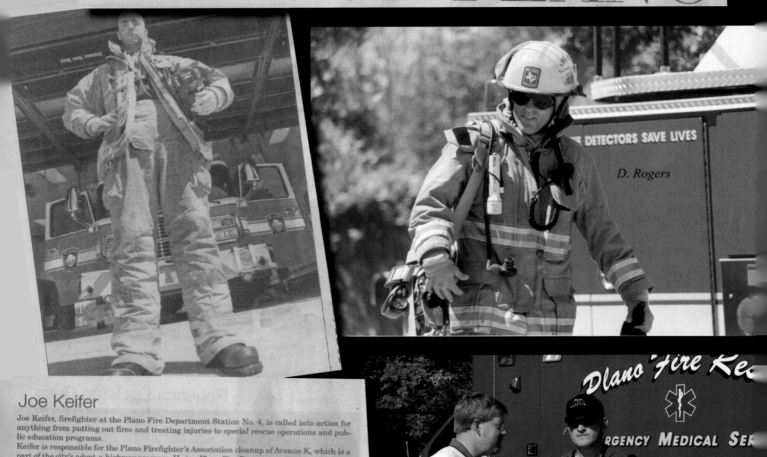

D. Rogers

Joe Keifer

Joe Keifer, firefighter at the Plano Fire Department Station No. 4, is called into action for anything from putting out fires and treating injuries to special rescue operations and public education programs.

Keifer is responsible for the Plano Firefighter's Association cleanup of Avenue K, which is a part of the city's adopt-a-highway program. He is a Plano Fire Department Explorer Program advisor, a program geared toward high school-aged kids who are interested in the fire service as a career.

Keifer believes it is always nice to give back to others.

He is married to his high school sweetheart and has a 2-year-old daughter. He moved to Plano in 1985 when he was 6 and started first grade at Carlisle Elementary and graduated from Plano Senior High School in 1997. He is a resident of McKinney now, but he believes Plano is a great city all around.

"It has excellent schools, good shopping, fantastic restaurants and is safe," he said.

Keifer went through the Citizen's Fire Academy in Plano right after high school and then the Explorers program before he went to the Texas Fire Training School at Texas A&M University. Once he graduated, he was hired on to Plano FD to fulfill his dream of being a firefighter.

Where there's smoke, there's fire
PFRA, Plano FD schedule smoke alarm program day

KIM WILLIAMS
kwilliams@acnpapers.com

A recent fire initiated a warm-weather proactive prevention event: installing smoke alarms for residents who may not have them.

After the Plano Fire Department responded to a manufactured home structure fire at a local mobile home park, Fire Safety Coordinator Capt. Peggy Harrell decided to schedule a smoke alarm program day, even though the temperature was sweltering.

"I try to make it cooler on the days we go out," Harrell said. "That day, it was so hot outside — but I thought the community could benefit from the smoke alarm program while the images of the fire were still fresh in all the residents' minds."

On July 5, residents had escaped the fire without injury; however, an investigation revealed that there were no working smoke alarms in that home.

Jonathan Sennetti, president of the Plano Fire Rescue Associates, said fire chiefs immediately became concerned that there may be other mobile homes within the park that didn't have working smoke alarms.

"In preparation for the program, PFRA members Bettye Phillips and Barb Homrighausen teamed up with Harrell and PFD Operations Assistant Chief Alan Storck," said Sennetti.

"They pre-walked the entire community on Thursday, hanging flyers on each door which notified the residents of the upcoming program. Then on Saturday morning, it was time for action," Sennetti said.

Thirteen PFRA members showed up ready to walk, despite the summer heat approaching 100 degrees."

PFRA members paired up with firefighters from PFD Engine 3, Medic 3 and Truck 8, as well as Harrell and PFD Chief Hugo Esparza. Teams of two knocked on the doors of more than 150 mobile homes and were able to test and verify smoke alarms for 105 residents.

"Most residents did have smoke alarms; however, many of those units had dead batteries, which left them as vulnerable as homes that had no smoke alarm at all," Sennetti said. "The teams ended up replacing 151 batteries in old alarms, and they installed 54 new smoke alarms across the 105 homes. Two of these alarms were special units equipped with strobe lights, which were installed in a home with deaf residents."

While inside each home, PFRA members discussed the importance of smoke alarms with the residents, provided them with a fire-safety checklist and answered questions.

"All of the PFRA members who volunteered for this quickly organized smoke alarm door-to-door event were hot and exhausted but very proud to have participated," said Sennetti. "The Plano Fire Department also recognized the importance of this event, and they expressed appreciation to PFRA for their side-by-side assistance."

"PFRA looks forward to participating with the Plano Fire Department in the next smoke alarm door-to-door event as well as their other fire-prevention programs that help keep the city of Plano and its citizens safe," said Sennetti.

"The PFD has been doing this door-to-door campaign since 1996," Harrell said. "The last two years, PFRA has been assisting us with it. This allows us to use less firefighters from the station and team them up with a volunteer."

The campaign is usually implemented three times a year but can be implemented whenever it is needed.

PFRA is a local fire corps program of citizen volunteers who donate their time, skills and talents with education and awareness activities that support and assist the PFD and its firefighters in their efforts to promote fire and life safety. It has more than 50 active members and was founded in 1995 for the purpose of raising funds to support the PFD annual awards banquet.

SUBMITTED PHOTO
Captain Randy Stone and FRS Kyle Crayton install a new smoke alarm.

Fire hits apartments

BILL CONRAD / STAFF PHOTO

No injuries were reported in the one-alarm apartment fire in east Plano Friday.

No one injured as 8 units burn

BILL CONRAD

bconrad@acnpapers.com

A fire engulfed building 14 of the Waterford on the Meadow apartments Friday night. The complex is located at the intersection of Shiloh Road and 14th Street in southeast Plano.

Firefighters from Fire Station 3 responded to multiple 911 calls about 11:15 p.m. First responders entered the building and firefighters and policemen began evacuating residents in building 14 as well as surrounding buildings.

"The firemen fought the fire from the interior but got reports of a falling ceiling inside the building, so they pulled out and started fighting the fire defensively," said Captain Peggy Harrell of the Plano Fire Department.

Harrell said that by fighting the fire defensively, firefighters kept the fire confined to building 14.

There are 16 apartments in the building and Harrell said eight have fire damage, but all 16 have extensive smoke and water damage.

Residents of the complex said after they were evacuated, they went outside and saw a chimney in building 14 explode as well as flames coming out of the roof of the second-story units.

Harrell said four fire engines, two fire trucks and two medical units responded to the call.

According to Harrell, all residents of the building were told to report to the leasing office, from where, she believed, they would be relocated to empty apartments.

FIRE

2000-2011

RESCUE

"Thirty years later..."

FIRE
2000-2011
RESCUE

"On September 11, 2001, in merely a few minutes, our country was changed for all time. The attacks weren't on a faceless infrastructure. They were on our neighbors, our friends and our families. That's how a firefighter sees it. This is why 343 of my Brothers and Sisters made the ultimate sacrifice. Still today that number is climbing. We aren't motivated by money, fame or glory. Instead, we ask 'if not us, then who? If not now, then when?'"

~ Floyd Jones,
Captain

STARLOCALNEWS.COM

plano★star courier *sunday*

VOLUME 121, NO. 185

SEPTEMBER 12, 2010

Sept. 11 Memorial

Never forgetting the fallen

ZACH MARKOVIC

Members of the Plano Firefighters Pipe and Drum team salute and honor those who were killed in the Sept. 11 attacks.

ACKNOWLEDGEMENTS

Hugo Esparza, Fire Chief
Mark Gamber, Medical Director
Peggy Harrell, Captain
Cynthia Morgan, Administrative Coordinator
Justin Samuel, Fire Rescue Specialist

Bob Acker, Assistant Chief, Retired
Jimmy Bell, Captain, Retired
Carl Dane, Captain, Retired
Jimmy Davidson, Captain, Retired
Paul Mayfield, Assistant Chief, Retired
Kirk Owen, Assistant Chief, Retired

Sylvia Berry, Senior Administrative Assistant, City of Plano Records Management

Cheryl Smith, Genealogy Librarian, Genealogy, Local History, Texana, and Archives, City of Plano Public Library System

Deborah Stone, Public Information
Supervisor, City of Plano Public Information

Barbara Gunter, Daughter of Retired Plano Captain Eldon Dyer

George "Beano" Gunter, Plano volunteer firefighter 1960 -1973

Jim Landers, Nephew of Cotton Landers and son of former Plano volunteer firefighter, Cletus Landers

Cynthia Hudson Reed, Granddaughter of Gee Hudson, Plano Fire Chief 1911-1920

Plano Fire Rescue Associates, Inc.
Plano Fire Fighters Association, Local 2149

Plano Star Courier Archives

Dallas Morning News Archives

Plano, Texas The Early Years, Friends of the Plano Public Library

"One day this job will be done with me, it's the way of things. For as long as the blood runs warm in my veins, however, I will never be done with the job. That's the seldom spoken sentiment of most firefighters. It keeps us running in when others are running out, even when we know the odds are stacked against us. As my career winds down it gives me great pride to look upon the eager young faces of the next generation of firefighters who will pick up the gauntlet. I can promise you that they will not fail you, because they are me and I am them. We are family. We are American Firefighters."

~ *Floyd Jones,*
Captain

Over the nine-month period this book was compiled, several never-before published photos were collected, found buried in the City's archival vaults or provided through the generosity of current and retired Plano Fire Department personnel and families.

It is our hope this publication will not only be a portal to the past but a springboard for future generations of Plano firefighters who one day will gaze upon the next 125 years of service provided to the community through a similar publication.

We encourage every person with a vested interest in the Plano Fire Department to collect and preserve photos and memorabilia so the history being made today may be enjoyed in the future.

Captain Peggy Harrell   Deborah Stone
Editor   Editor